THE REAL POWER
OF BRANDS

THE
REAL POWER
OF BRANDS

Making brands work for competitive advantage

Stuart Crainer

FT

PITMAN
PUBLISHING

PITMAN PUBLISHING
128 Long Acre, London WC2E 9AN

A Division of Pearson Professional Limited

First published in Great Britain 1995

British Library Cataloguing in Publication Data
A CIP catalogue record for this book can be obtained
from the British Library.

ISBN 0 273 61379 0

1 3 5 7 9 10 8 6 4 2

Typeset by Northern Phototypesetting Co. Ltd., Bolton
Printed and bound in Great Britain by
Biddles Ltd, Guildford and King's Lynn

*The Publishers' policy is to use paper manufactured
from sustainable forests.*

CONTENTS

INTRODUCTION

In the hyper-competition of the 1990s, no business or management practice is sacrosanct. The decade so far has seen the slaying of the corporate equivalent of sacred cows. Jobs are no longer for life; expertise is outsourced and people are employed on a project-by-project basis. Great swathes have been cut through what was once the safest area of all: middle management. In a relentless flurry of down-sizing and right-sizing, change is sweeping the business community. No business or manager can escape the consequences.

A new world order is emerging. It is based round insecurity, uncertainty and ambiguity. The scale of the new environment is no longer geographically limited. Instead, it is global and highly complex.

But what does this have to do with brands?

The impact of the massive changes now underway affects brands and those who manage them in a variety of different ways. First, brands are dealing with many of the same global issues which are dominating other corporate agendas. Brands in the 1990s are a global phenomenon.

Second, the way brands are managed is undergoing radical change in many organisations. If best management practice must change to fit the new world order so, too, must brand management. If an organisation embraces re-engineering it can't ignore the fact that brand management is a vital activity which often benefits from the rigorous examination which re-engineering demands. Brand management cannot be isolated from the rest of the organisation.

Third, brands are emerging as a vital competitive weapon in a huge number of industries and businesses. If companies are to thrive in the future they need to make use of every competitive weapon at their disposal. To overlook the commercial importance of brands is a luxury none can now afford.

The real power of brands lies in their competitive potential. They can drive businesses forward, transform them, differentiate them and, in some cases, save them from extinction. Approaching the millennium, recognising and harnessing the power and value of brands is a corporate necessity.

Stuart Crainer
May 1995

1

IN A WORLD WITHOUT NAMES

Following years of cruel captivity, one of the Beirut hostages stumbled down the road after being released by his captors in the middle of the war-torn city and was eventually picked up by a passing car. He explained who he was and then added: 'I could really do with a Heineken.'

After being held captive for a lengthy period, the former hostage still remembered the brand name. Indeed, all thoughts of the product were secondary to the brand name. This, above all, was a triumph for Heineken's brand managers and advertising agency. After years of sensory deprivation the brand was so strongly imprinted on the hostage's mind to come, immediately and automatically, to his lips. (Even if you are sceptical and believe the story is probably apocryphal it is worth thinking about why it became so widely told.)

BRAND LOYALTY

Such brand loyalty and recall is no longer surprising, though few other consumers have ever been so tested. Brands are an ever-present part of our lives – from the clothes we wear, to the food we eat; from the toys our children play with, to the drinks we consume; from our mobile phones to our cigarettes. We read about brands in our carefully branded newspapers. Brands are even newsworthy – on a typical day early in 1995 someone in the West Midlands named their baby son after a brand, Nike; a brand of beer called Cantona Bitter was launched; and a Tyneside beer drinker was granted his final wish – his ashes were scattered in the grounds of Scottish and

Brands are an ever-present part of our lives – from the clothes we wear, to the food we eat; from the toys our children play with, to the drinks we consume; from our mobile phones to our cigarettes.

Newcastle Breweries and mixed with a bottle of Newcastle Brown Ale.

Brand loyalty appears to know no bounds and almost everything appears to be capable of being branded: turkeys (thanks to Bernard Matthews), bananas (Geest), water (Evian et al.), soccer teams (Manchester United) and even drain repairs (Dyno-Rod).

If you look around you now, how many brands can you see? Try to imagine a life without brands. Walking into a shop would pose a massive challenge to your powers of communication; instead of simply ordering a particular item, you would have to describe it in detail every time. Interestingly, when science fiction writers try to describe the robotic awfulness of their imaginary society one of the first things they do is remove all brand names. People are always distressed by the clinical absurdity of 'Snack One' and 'Drink Two' – they may be in an alien world but they expect a bag of Hula Hoops and a Seven Up.

Defiant to the end?

Of course, there is always the odd one out. Some products have yet to find their Bernard Matthews and have defied branding, so far:

● **The egg:** small and perfectly formed it may be, but the humble egg is apparently unbrandable. An egg is an egg. The nearest the egg has come to being branded was the 1960s advertising campaign in which various people went to work on an egg – these included soccer star George Best, not often celebrated for his capacity for hard work, early mornings or sensible breakfasts. More recently, there have been half-hearted attempts at introducing advertising on eggs. The trend towards free-range eggs has also created an opportunity, as yet unfulfilled, for a company to create the ultimate free-range brand.

- **Milk:** no organisation has successfully branded milk. Attempts to do so are persistent. Supermarkets now carry a wide variety of types of milk, including the curious and unexplainable 'breakfast' milk, without managing to attach a brand name to any of them. In the future we may express a preference for Unigate or Dairy Crest milk rather than Sainsbury's own label 'Classic Milk'.

- **Plumbing services:** plumbing should, in theory at least, be easy prey for the brand-loving organisation. Most of the jobs are fairly straightforward but sometimes unpleasant. The trouble is, for some reason, we prefer our small local plumber. We wouldn't feel comfortable calling in a global chain to sort out a broken cistern, this would seem too intrusive.

- **Oranges:** to some extent, apples have been successfully branded – we buy English Cox's or French Golden Delicious. Orange producers try equally hard but conspicuously fail. We may buy Uruguayan or Israeli oranges but are unlikely to actively seek them out.

THE SPREAD OF BRANDS

Some products will continue to escape, but brands are increasingly spreading their commercial tentacles in new directions. Countries are branded, as are regions and cities and even the Olympic Games now appears as much an exercise in brand management as athletic achievement. Individual people have also become brands. Yves St Laurent and Calvin Klein are real people who have metamorphosed into worldwide brands. Singers, groups and entertainers are brands. Take That come accompanied by a logo, product, corporate identity, sub-brands and sponsorship. The entertainer formerly known as Prince has taken branding a stage further by reducing himself to a symbol. It is difficult to determine whether this is a marketing ploy or a creative statement. Less frivolously, Harvard Business School professor Michael Porter who is a highly successful management thinker, author and consultant says he is aware of protecting and developing 'the Michael Porter brand'. He knows that if he spreads himself too thinly and attempts to do too many things, the source of his fame and renown i.e. his intellectual rigour and insight, will wither away. The brand may appear almighty but it still needs to be protected.

Not only has the world of brands expanded to take in virtually everything that can be made, provided or breathe, it has re-invented its traditional relationships. Take what was once a renowned but local beer, Boddingtons. Ten years ago, Boddingtons was to be found in the pubs of north-western England and nowhere else. Indeed, a pint of Boddingtons was rarely found even in Liverpool and, on discovering the cream of Manchester on Merseyside, it was customary to reflect that the beer didn't travel well.

Similarly, itinerant northerners were wont to complain about the poor quality of beers elsewhere and espouse the singular virtues of Boddingtons. They were highly persuasive. Today, Boddingtons can be found throughout the UK in pubs and on supermarket shelves. From being small and local, Boddingtons has become a nationally recognised brand complete with its own distinctive off-beat advertising and the obligatory range of T-shirts. A traditional beer has become a brand. It is likely that soon the world will have to come to terms with Boddingtons Light or a range of designer leisure wear featuring the Boddingtons colours.

Brands like Boddingtons are now commonplace. Small, locally available products have been converted into nationally and internationally renowned money-earners. Sleeping giants such as Lucozade, once only drunk under sufferance when you were ill, have been transformed into commercial success stories drunk by olympic athletes at every available photo opportunity.

The world of brands has expanded. Once it was dominated by fast-moving consumer goods. Now it is filled with retailers (from Kwik-Fit to St Michael, Dixons to Benneton) and financial services companies (banking services such as First Direct, building societies and insurers).

You might question whether the profusion of brands is necessarily a good thing. There is something discomforting about the great cities of the world, instant desserts, high-tech gadgets, drugs and filing cabinets all being brands. Does the hard sell and the carefully contrived image have to enter into every single activity on earth?

Unfortunately, or fortunately for some, branding is as inescapable a fact of life as the four seasons. If Shakespeare was writing *Romeo and Juliet* in the mid-1990s he would be thinking about product placement and defining characters by their favourite brands (Burberry, Caterpillar Boots and Sol lager for Romeo; Chanel, Hermes and Gucci for Juliet). This might in some quarters be seen as crass bad taste. But brands are little more than prompts, symbols and representations – concepts which have been used since we started buying and selling things. Brands are marketing shorthand which companies hope will lead us to purchase their particular products.

Brands have become associated with the hard-selling entrepreneurial superficiality of the 1980s when deals were everything and brands changed hands as readily as stolen watches. The 1990s have brought brands back to earth. Companies now appreciate that brands are neither frivolous nor a necessary evil, but important, expensive and potentially lucrative investments. That they are now all-embracing is a fact of life, caused in part by the human need for reassurance, labelling and ease of identity.

The appeal of brands

Brands are exciting. For business people and consumers, the world of brands appears invigorating and sometimes glamorous. It is the world of Bacardi advertisements and multi-million pound campaigns. But, there is much more to brands than this alluring image. There is also, for example, a comfort factor. Brands may pander to our dreams and aspirations – beaches, sunshine, not a worry in the world and a glass of spirits too – but they also reassure. We like the idea of a life of excitement and unlimited finance, but settle for having a drink in the comfort of our home. The brand becomes a surrogate for our ambitions and dreams. The successful brands are the ones which we are comfortable with, but which are not complacent. They sell us Caribbean dreams at an affordable price. We know what the brand does, what it looks like and how much it costs, and the best brands continually meet and exceed our expectations.

Dull though this sounds, people thrive on reassurance and they return again and again to places and products which they can trust. For example, I have just been to the supermarket. Before me at the checkout, a lady was buying a can of the cheapest beans. A new idea, they are absolutely minimalist – plain wrapper, no name, low price. The lady stopped to question the shop assistant: 'What are they like?' she asked. 'Alright, I've had them myself', said the shop assistant. Without a brand name, the lady felt unsure. The beans were cheap, very cheap, but what would they taste like? Without any of the usual reassuring reference points (name, logo, catchy phrase, packaging) it was as if she was buying the national dish of Venezuela rather than baked beans. Given a can of Heinz beans she would have expected them to taste, well, like beans; a brand-free can, however, comes without such reassurance, even though it is undoubtedly a fairly similar product.

Someone I know was setting up his own business. When he bought his computers he had a choice between a brand name he had never heard of and a widely known one. He chose the latter. 'I have a mental image of who my customers are,' he explains. 'They are impressed by good brand names. They want to see them and be reassured by their presence. My imagined customer would respond favourably to the sight of the brand I have chosen.' By being associated with good brand names, he believes some of these positive perceptions will influence the way his customers view his business.

Brands are powerful weapons. Some even force themselves deep into the psyche of entire nations. Vegemite is an Australian cultural icon, as essential to the rearing of young Australians as their mother's milk. The Italian love affair with Nutella is a similarly curious phenomenon – and one likely to keep psychologists at work for many years to come. The tasty chocolate spread has been celebrated for its cultural impact by Umberto Eco and, in a survey of the sexual fantasies of young Italians, was mentioned repeatedly. Nutella's maker, Ferrero, enigmatically describes its product as 'the physical sublimation of chocolate'.

What is a brand?

So, if mere association with a brand name can be a commercial weapon and brands can entrance entire nations, what actually is a brand? Although we mention, come across and invest in brand names every day of our lives (try driving down a street in any town or city without encountering a brand name) actually explaining what a brand is and what it does is usually taken for granted. In fact, our entire conception of what a brand is and does (as well as how much it is worth) is fast evolving.

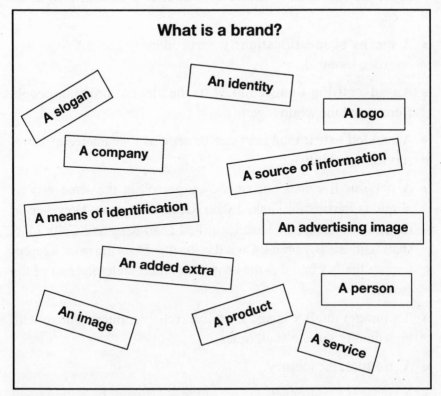

Figure 1.1   Elements of a brand

Think of an individual company. Take British Airways as an example. In fact the BA brand encompasses all of the elements listed in Figure 1.1. BA is a company, a legal entity; the real BA is the brand. The BA brand includes:

- **A slogan:** *'The world's favourite airline'*.

- **An identity:** this includes the uniforms worn by its staff; the appearance of offices and ticket desks; plane exteriors and interiors.

- **A logo:** simple and distinctive, half of a red arrow.

- **A company:** BA the corporate brand is backed by sub-brands such as Concorde, Club Class, Club Europe etc.

- **A source of information:** travelling with BA says something about the consumer – obviously it is often a statement of affluence.

- **A means of identification:** we can identify the BA logo in a crowded terminal.

- **An advertising image:** linked to the slogan; bringing people from round the world together.

- **An added extra:** the brand can be seen as a guarantee of better service, reliability etc.

- **A person:** BA does not embody a person in the same way as Virgin is inextricably linked with Richard Branson. However, in the 1980s some might have identified Lord King and Colin Marshall with the BA brand. On a day-to-day basis the person representing the BA brand is the hostess or ticket seller in front of the customer.

- **An image:** the BA image is stylish, reliable, international, with high quality service at all times.

- **A product:** the journey.

- **A service:** the strongest aspect of the BA brand. Its selling point is its dedication to service.

It is notable that this is very wide-ranging and that the product, while being vital, is not all-important. BA the brand is about more than a flight. Similarly, Heineken the brand is more than a beer; it is something that stays in your minds and is not easily dislodged.

2

WHAT IS A BRAND?

CHARACTERISTICS OF A BRAND

A brand is likely to contain nearly all the following elements … and many, many more.

The brand states ownership

At its simplest, branding is a statement of ownership. Cows are branded and, in the commercial world, branding can be traced back to trademarks placed on Greek pots in the seventh century BC and, later, to medieval tradesmen who put trademarks on their products to protect themselves and buyers against inferior imitations. (Of course, in the modern world people are adept at copying trademarks – whether they are Lacoste, Sony, Rolex or Le Coq Sportif – and producing imitations, which are often highly accurate.)

Trademarks remain highly effective prompts – there are now some 50 million registered worldwide. The first trademark registered in the UK was the red triangle used for Bass beer. Other well-known ones include the Woolmark symbol, Tate & Lyle's sugar cube and the arch-like McDonald's 'M'. The image of a dog listening to a record being played on a phonograph was originally bought from the painter by the managing director of the Gramophone Company. Unable to register the name 'gramophone' as a trademark as it was already a generic term, the managing director registered his favourite painting as his trademark. His Master's Voice was created, and later recreated as HMV, though still with the musically appreciative dog.

Such symbols now act as a kind of shorthand. As soon as you see them your mind thinks of the brand. Interestingly, their meaning is relatively unimportant. The HMV dog continues to be used even though the company has changed fundamentally in size and nature. Its target audience is young and fashion-conscious, yet the dated symbol continues to be used and is, presumably, effective.

The brand is a product

John Pemberton's brain tonic contained a leaf from a South American tree and West African seeds as well as caramel, phosphoric acid and a combination of seven 'natural flavours' which remains a well-protected secret to this day. He named it Coca-Cola.

In the beginning came the product. Branding was a mark on the product – a signature or symbol – signifying its origin or ownership. The traditional view of what constitutes a brand is shown in Figure 2.1 and summed up by marketing guru Philip Kotler in his classic textbook *Marketing Management*. Kotler writes:

> '[A brand name is] a name, term, sign, symbol or design, or a combination of these, which is intended to identify the goods or services of one group of sellers and differentiate them from those of competitors.'[1]

The trouble with older definitions of brands is that they remain pre-occupied with the physical product. The product stands alone; the brand exists within corporate ether. The product comes first and the brand does little more than make it clear which company made the product and where. John Pemberton's brain tonic is the product, but the brand is much more.

A more recent definition comes from Richard Koch in his book *The Financial Times A-Z of Management and Finance*.[2] Koch defines a brand as:

> 'A visual design and/or name that is given to a product or service by an organisation in order to differentiate it from competing products and which assures consumers that the product will be of high and consistent quality.'

Reflecting the emphasis of our times, Koch stresses differentiation i.e. making your product or service different (or seeming to be different), and achieving consistent quality.

'Good products don't make winners; winners make good products', say James Champy and Michael Hammer in *Re-engineering the Corporation.*[3] If a company divides itself along product lines few eyebrows are raised. A building society, for example, divided its operations into separate businesses in the 1980s. These included mortgages, life policies and credit cards. Though it appears to be a logical thing to do, the problem is that the fascination with products overlooks customers who are not so easily separated. A single customer may take out a mortgage and a life policy and want another credit card. They would prefer to be able to deal with a single entity rather than being passed from one product division to another.

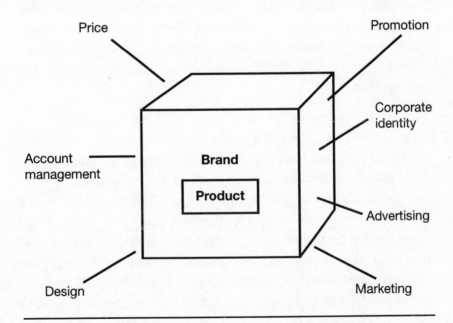

Figure 2.1   The brand as product

A faith in good products leading to competitiveness is long-established. Yet, time and time again innovative products have failed to yield the anticipated financial results. Other companies quickly copy new ideas or produce their own versions of the product. With time-cycles diminishing this is more efficiently done than ever before. Organisations can no longer rely on a new product reaping huge dividends over a lengthy period as competitors try and make up the lost ground. Products are now easily copied and retain their uniqueness for a shorter and shorter time. In contrast, brands can maintain their originality and freshness.

The brand provides information

'The point of brands is, and always has been, to provide information. The form of that information varies from market to market, and from time to time. Some products make a visible statement about their users' style, modernity or wealth – examples include clothes, cars and accessories. Others purport to convey reliability, say, or familiarity, or something else. Whatever the information, however, the right question to ask is this: does the buyer still need or want it?', acutely observed a 1994 editorial in The Economist. [4]

It is easy to underestimate the amount of information a brand contains. There is the physical information (the contents, ingredients, weight, calorific content) and there is the abstract information (the statements about the user, the associations, the memories).

If you don't believe that brands can be informative take a jar of Bovril. This is a truly wonderful brand. Twenty years ago, Bovril was a watery drink you drank at half-time during wintry football matches. It was an old-fashioned product at home in the miserable milieu of fourth division football grounds. If someone had told you, as you painfully forced boiling fluid past chapped lips, that someone like Jerry Hall would be advertising Bovril in a few years time you would have expressed surprise to say the least. You would also be astonished when told that Ms Hall's punchline was her claim to possess a 'Bovril body'.

Despite such glamorous advertising, the jar of Bovril is crowded with information (see Figure 2.2). Not all of it is spelt out (though the word 'Bovril' manages to feature eight times). Information comes in a variety of forms: the packaging tells us something (Bovril is stout and substantial, while being of manageable size); as do our feelings about the product (traditional, warming, savoury). The Bovril brand, therefore, is a rich mixture of the product (same as it ever was); the advertising (surprising); the packaging (traditional but not dated); physical appearance (robust) and our feelings and expectations.

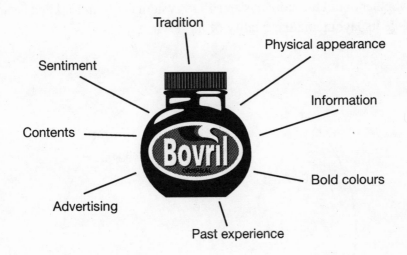

Figure 2.2 The Bovril brand

The brand is an experience

With hyper-competition and constant change, companies have sought to extract more financial worth from their brands. Traditional definitions and the approaches they embody have tended to look a little limiting. Who wants Bovril as a warming drink? And, who wants Bovril as a multi-purpose, low fat, cleverly advertised, brand for the 1990s?

Increasingly, people's perception of what constitutes a brand is widening. Instead of being sacrosanct and untouchable, the product is beginning to be regarded as just one element of the brand. While in the past the product came first and other elements followed, now the product is a single component of the marketing mix alongside price, promotion and distribution (see Figure 2.3).

Some idea of the complexity of modern brands can be seen by looking at retail brands such as Sainsbury and Marks & Spencer in the UK. The total Sainsbury or M&S brand is made up of not only the store, its location and contents (size of product range etc.), but also the quality of service, range of own-label products, price competitiveness and even trading hours. The brand is all-embracing – whether or not the store has an EPOS system is a brand-related issue, as is its layout and the quality of its service.

Figure 2.3   The new brand

The product is now recognised as only part of what the consumer **experiences** of the total brand. Note the emphasis on experience – customers used to buy things, now they experience them. We are in a new era, where brands are viewed as having emotional and lifestyle benefits which are transferable across several products, rather than being narrowly identified with a particular product.

'Brands, as the better marketers have come to realise, do not really belong to the manufacturer. They belong to the consumer', says Paul Southgate in *Total Branding by Design*.[5] At this point, managers may throw their arms in the air. For many, consumer control is as acceptable as the lunatics taking over the asylum.

Brands **are** driven by consumers. They are psychological, as well as physical.

> *'Brands enable consumers to identify products or services which promise specific benefits. They arouse expectations in the minds of customers about quality, price, purpose and performance,'*

says J. Hugh Davidson in *Offensive Marketing*. Brands are about hearts and minds.

A French consultancy, Desgrippes Cato Gobé, even has a research tool called SENSE (Sensory Exploration and Need States Evaluation) which examines the psyche of customers and attempts to match it with the visual image of a brand.

> *'We believe not in pushing products onto customers but, by understanding more about what the customers want, pulling them almost subconsciously towards the products',*

says the company's founder and partner Mac Cato.

The move from product to psychology is a huge leap. How does an experience differ from a purchase? It is largely a matter of perception and interpretation. Take a pint of Boddingtons bought in a pub. A pint of Boddingtons is the product; the Boddingtons brand, however, brings in all the various factors which distinguish, differentiate and characterise it. The brand encompasses the way it is marketed, promoted, packaged, distributed and presented, as well as the end product.

So, the humble pint (the product) is surrounded by prompts and persuasion. There is mass media, advertising (the witty captions about the cream of Manchester); and the environment (the pub with its array of Boddingtons beer-mats, towels, T-shirts, calendars, mirrors, ashtrays and more). If you throw in the added complexity of our own feelings and perceptions – does Boddingtons make us feel part of something? – then you begin to understand the confusing nature of the modern brand.

To look at the product in isolation from the overall package is no longer possible; the simple purchase is perceived as an experience. 'We tend to perceive things more easily as representatives of categories than in their own right, as unique and idiosyncratic', concluded psychologist Abraham Maslow in *Motivation and Personality*. We are quite comfortable with bringing a wider perspective to a simple purchase, indeed, it can be reassuring as we sip our beer to realise that people are drinking the very same product in a very similar environment elsewhere. It has become mass participation. The trouble is that sometimes it feels like it.

While there is clearly more to a purchase than the simple exchange of money, a product-based concept of the brand is easily understood. A broader definition brings in a whole range of attributes which make up a brand – these may be real or illusory, rational or emotional, tangible or invisible. These attributes can emanate from one, all, or a combination of marketing mix elements. Viewing a brand in broader terms does make any consideration of brands more complex. But it is also more realistic because brands never were straightforward.

As well as various definitions as to what a brand is and does, brands have traditionally been broken down into different basic types:

- **Consumer goods brands:** Macleans, Lucozade, Coca-Cola.
- **Industrial brands:** Pilkington Glass.
- **Service brands:** InterCity, Kwik-Fit.
- **Corporate brands:** BP, IBM, M&S, Tesco, Benneton.

Such typecasting is increasingly redundant. In a world of brand profusion the dividing lines are no longer clear. Brands overlap and interact continuously. The category they belong to is not important, what matters is how they add value to what consumers experience and to the organisation.

Old	New
• The product	• The product and much more
• Physical	• Psychological
• Narrow	• Broad
• Purchase	• Experience
• The incidental customer	• The controlling consumer
• Reality	• Reality and illusion
• Isolation	• Interaction

Figure 2.4 The new world of brands

The brand is delicate: handle with care

The world may be increasingly filled with brands of all types, shapes and sizes, but it is also cluttered with expensive brand disasters. Quantity does not usually increase quality. Brands may be big and brash, but they are also delicate: managers and organisations must handle them with care.

Take one example. Schlitz is an American beer. It is now found only occasionally among the mass of taps bearing the logos Budweiser, Miller, Molston and the like. But in 1974 Schlitz was America's second most popular brand of beer. It held 16.1 per cent of the massive American market and appeared destined for a comfortable long life. Then the brewers introduced a revolutionary new process, 'accelerated batch fermentation'. This saved time and money. It appeared a triumph for all concerned. The beer tasted the same, what else could matter?

The problem was that customers didn't have faith in the new process. They believed the beer was below the standard they had come to expect – it tasted the same, but customers believed it wasn't the same. Schlitz's market share fell to less than a single percentage mark and the value of its name declined from in excess of $1 billion in 1974 to around $75 million in 1980.

Similarly, in 1985 Coca-Cola announced to the world that it was replacing its traditional cola with New Coke. In detailed research it had discovered that the new recipe was preferred by most consumers. It was, they said, smoother, sweeter and preferable to the old version. This conveniently overlooked the fact that the old version was selling in many millions every day of the week. To call this the marketing own goal of the century would be to overstate the effect only slightly. Coke was faced with a barrage of criticism. On the other hand, its arch-rival Pepsi could barely contain its glee, indeed, it quickly produced advertising which was extremely gleeful, rubbing in the fact that 'the real thing' remained unchanged.

Realising that its move had been disastrous, Coke backtracked and reintroduced the original coke. It has not been tinkered with since.

More farcical was the demise of the Ratners brand. Ratners, a chain of jewellers in the UK, suffered a form of corporate hari-kari when its chairman Gerald Ratner informed an august gathering at the Institute of Directors annual conference that its products were 'total crap'. Ratner's sales dropped by more than a third and the group (minus Mr Ratner) became re-christened as Signet.

Schlitz, Coke and Ratner's all demonstrated one thing in common: they forgot about consumers. All were (one remains) strong brands. But they all either treated customers with disdain (Ratner) or missed them out of their neat commercial equations (Schlitz and Coke).

Brands RIP

Brands come and go, but even those which are long departed remain fixed uneasily in our minds:

● **Double Diamond:** the beer which, its advertising boasted, 'worked wonders' couldn't actually work wonders on its own sales charts. Notable for the use of the word diamond – in theory, a good name for a premium brand, but one that has an indifferent track record compared to 'gold' – and the rather crass use of 'double' suggesting value for money and luxury in a single name.

- **Woodbines:** prior to the 1960s no-one smoked anything other than Woodbines. Lethal to children at five paces, Woodbines were cigarettes of legendary strength. In the age before brand extensions, their shelf life was shortened by the arrival of cheap and fashionable American brands. If Woodbines were alive today they would be marketed as Woodbines Light and Extra Light.

- **Watney's Red Barrel:** in the 1970s no party worthy of the name was complete without a large tin of Watney's Red Barrel (a Party Five). In a market replete with tradition, Watney's appeared too much of a bright young interloper – even sponsoring football tournaments. From a position of dominance, Watney's fell from grace in the face of competition from lager.

- **Tide:** the Daz of yesteryear. Tide conjured up images of the seashore and crystal clear seas. Such idyllic nonsense clearly bears little relation to the mundane act of washing clothes. Consumers weren't convinced. Now, detergents have suitably meaningless names with no nautical images.

The brand is robust

Brands have to be managed sensibly and cautiously otherwise they can fall to pieces in your hands. No-one can sit still – even Moet & Chandon is now advertising (its first UK campaign costing £1 million was launched in November 1994). On the other hand, they can be incredibly robust defying any notion of product or market maturity. The best brands go on and on, outlasting fads and competitors.

Notes

[1] Kotler, P., *Marketing Management: Analysis, Planning and Control* (8th edition), Prentice Hall, Englewood Cliffs, 1993.
[2] Koch, R., *The Financial Times A-Z of Management and Finance*, Pitman, London, 1994.

[3] Champy, J., & Hammer, M., *Re-engineering the Corporation*, Nicholas Brealey, London, 1993.
[4] 'Don't get left on the shelf', *The Economist*, 2 July 1994.
[5] Southgate, P., *Total Branding by Design*, Kogan Page, 1994.

3

A SHORT HISTORY OF BRANDS

INTRODUCTION

If we think of brands we inevitably begin with the great American brands: Marlboro, Coca-Cola, McDonald's, Budweiser and many, many more. They are the garish, colourful icons of our times. Many have become cultural touchstones. In Communist countries, the symbol of the West in the 1980s was a pair of Levis rather than the Statue of Liberty. Artists include brands in their work as symbols of our decadence, ignorance, tastelessness or as celebrations of our culture.

Our image of these great icons often bears little relation to the product or reality. Wearing a pair of Levis does not give you freedom. We think, for example, of Greyhound buses as bullet-grey, speeding through the night along wide and straight highways. Yet, most people have probably never been on a Greyhound bus or even seen one. If they had, they might think twice about taking any journey and any vision of it speeding anywhere would quickly be questioned – Greyhounds stop at the most out of the way hamlets imaginable.

Similarly, the red and white Marlboro packet evokes images of cowboys (created by the company's advertisers) and freedom. Instead of thinking here is an addictive, health-

> **The brand can defeat reality.**

damaging product, we dream of a vision created by advertising executives. The brand can defeat reality.

Brands become embedded in our minds, but we not only remember the names, we also recall the characteristics the brands would like to be associated with (see Figure 3.1).

Try to match the brand with the description:

Haagen-Daz	mild
Stella Artois	popular
Halifax Building Society	reliable
Fairy Liquid	sensual
Coca-Cola	high quality
British Airways	refreshing
AA	international
Hanson	helpful

Figure 3.1 Brand association

That the iconic brands of the twentieth century are American owes a great deal to the fact that American businesses have continually developed brands at a faster pace than their European counterparts. This can partly be attributed to geography. American companies had (and have) a huge homogeneous national market; Europe does not. While American companies could launch massive advertising and marketing campaigns across the US and the English-speaking world, European companies learned to adapt (or not) to the cultural nuances of individual countries.

Curing all-known ills

Trailers once travelled the American countryside laden with every possible known cure, stimulant, medicine or treatment. The medicine jamborees may have had an indifferent medical record, but their contribution to the success of brands cannot be overlooked. They played a small but significant part in the development of national branding during the late nineteenth century. Patent medicines and tobacco set the trend. Though distributed only region-ally, they developed recognisable brand names and identities.

The increase of brands on a regional basis provided the foundation for growth on a much greater scale. Instead of being restricted to low quality, regionally distributed products, brands took the great leap forward into the high quality mass market. The conditions were fertile. Efficient pan-American transportation had emerged so that a successful product in Chicago could be sold in St Louis cost-effectively.

But improvements weren't limited to transport, production processes and packaging improved and advertising became almost respectable. There were also changes in trademark laws and increasing industrialisation and urbanisation. While the brands expanded, their management remained resolutely set in its ways. Company owners and directors took responsibility. The array of tools at their disposal – from premiums and free samples, to mass advertising – grew quickly.

The period after the First World War cemented the position of brands. Advertising became increasingly prevalent and the acquisition of brands became identified with success and development. Consumers wanted Fords not motor cars; they bought from Sears rather than elsewhere.

Brand management

Success brought complexity. Companies began to own a number of brands which they were able to produce, distribute and sell en masse. Complexity encouraged the functional division of labour, through production lines with workers performing repetitious tasks on a mammoth scale, and the functional division of management. Management became separated into different functions such as marketing, sales, R&D and production. The separation was ruthlessly enforced. 'It is not necessary for any one department to know what any other department is doing', Henry Ford propounded. 'It is the business of those who plan the entire work to see that all of the departments are working ... towards the same end.' Ford believed that managers should work in isolation, unencumbered by the problems of their colleagues, simply concentrating on what they were employed to do.

The downside of such 'scientific' management is now well known and accepted. Ruthlessly satirised by Charlie Chaplin in *Modern Times*, such 'science' brought with it worker alienation, a lack of co-ordination between different functions and a complete absence of flexibility. Any sense of individual responsibility was sucked away by the system. Imaginations were never stretched; intelligence was not developed.

In 1931, Procter & Gamble took functional organisation a stage further when it created a new function: brand management. With brands like Ivory and Camay bath soaps, P&G believed that the best way to organise itself would be to give responsibility to a single individual: a brand manager.

The system did not transform the world overnight, but gradually brand management became an accepted functional activity, an adjunct to sales and marketing and often a fairly junior adjunct at that. Its popularity was fuelled by the economic boom of the 1950s which produced a plethora of new products and brands. These were supplemented by developments such as shopping centres and the emergence of television advertising. We had never had it so good and never had so much. Brand management provided some hope of order amid the confusion introduced by prosperity.

By 1967, 84 per cent of large manufacturers of consumer packaged goods in the United States had brand managers. Though titles have changed, this system largely prevails today. It is only in the 1990s that the brand management system has begun to be questioned through trends such as re-engineering which seeks to break down the long-established functional barriers.

The effectiveness of brands

As you wait in the queue at the supermarket checkout it is tempting and diverting to analyse the contents of someone else's shopping basket. You examine the conveyor belt as it travels along carrying the secrets of someone's food, drink and brand consumption. As you see the brands you draw conclusions about a person's habits, tastes and means. For better or worse (probably the latter) brands say something about us (see Figure 3.2).

Brands produce stereotypes. Take the following examples of the brands two imaginary people buy:

        Consumer 1:   Hunter – wellingtons
                              Volvo – car
                              Gianni Versace – clothes
                              Rolex – watch
                              Moet & Chandon – drink

        Consumer 2:   Mazda – car
                              Hush Puppies – shoes
                              Burtons – clothes
                              Sharp – watch
                              Tetley – drink

In fact, these shortlists produce two stereotypical men. This does not tell us anything about them as people, but the fact that the stereotypes are so strong says a great deal about the effectiveness of branding. We are not what we consume, but brand managers and companies would like us to believe we are.

Figure 3.2 We are not what we consume

Food thoughts

The development of food brands reveals many of the important stages in the development of brands as a whole. The origins of some of the world's largest food brands lie in the nineteenth century when the likes of Heinz and Nestlé created a vast new market in mass produced food. Heinz set off 'To do the common thing uncommonly well'. He and his company did so with uncommon success – Heinz's sales were $6.6 billion in 1992.

Having invented the market, the companies realised that its parameters were increasingly evident. In response to the simple fact that there's a limit to how much people can eat, the companies shifted their attention to value-added products to which they could attach premium prices. The emphasis was on pre-packed meals, eating healthily, speed and efficiency. A myriad of different brands and segments emerged. Consumers wanted to eat tasty, healthy food. They wanted it pre-prepared, ready and easy to cook.

> **We are not what we consume, but brand managers and companies would like us to believe we are.**

The result was a massive market. In 1992 one estimate put the global sales of packaged food at $2.8 trillion. Huge profits and cash reserves meant that the companies could afford to buy brands from other areas of the food business. In the 1980s there was a steady stream of mergers and acquisitions. Enormous amounts of money and huge numbers of brands changed hands.

As is always the case, even in the world of booming brand budgets, reality returns. As premium prices increased, budgets mushroomed and the value of brands headed towards the commercial stratosphere, but consumers began to become a little reticent. They looked elsewhere and began to concentrate on value for money and the hard facts beyond the marketing.

Supermarkets quickly moved to take advantage of this change in emphasis through developing their own brands which had grown, but not hugely, in the previous decades. From having a 23 per cent share of packaged grocery turnover in 1978, own-label goods rose to 34.9 per cent in 1991. Indeed, research by the Henley Centre found that 'best' brands are now often retailers' own brands. The leading Dutch supermarket chain Albert Heijn's own-label products were ranked far ahead of Nestlé on all criteria, including trustworthiness, product innovation and packaging as well as price. The wheel has turned full circle. Indeed, the UK chain Tesco is now contemplating buying directly from farmers in another effort to increase profit margins.

The end result is that the market is now in a state of uncomfortable flux. Competition is intense, in a way that it has never been before when the food companies called the shots. The common link is that the process of change is led and formed by brands.

Matters of life and death

The new and emerging issues facing brands are, for many, a matter of life and death and include the following:

Fragmentation

Thanks to the likes of Heinz and Nestlé, markets have become highly fragmented. This means that there is always the possibility of an interloper stealing a march on bigger rivals by finding a small and lucrative niche. In recent years we have seen Sol creating a profitable niche in the lager market and many others have followed suit.

Targeting

The obvious repercussion of this is that targeting the right market and then the right part of that market is crucial. A large amount of information is now available on buying habits as well as a host of other factors. The only problem for organisations is how to plough through all the data to find the right information and at the same time move speedily to fill smaller and smaller niches.

Innovation and speed

The answer in many markets is to develop new products and services more quickly than has ever been done before. This means that development times have to be slashed. The big brands of recent years have been those which deluge the market with new ideas – companies like Compaq, Rubbermaid (which boasts a new product every day) and Swatch.

Cost squeeze

To make matters more challenging, organisations have to achieve
these things within reduced budgets. Gone are the days when a brand
could be pushed to the top simply through an expensive advertising
campaign. Consumers are more sophisticated and advertising costs
have soared. Even a household name like Unilever's Persil only has
around 25 per cent of its past amount of television advertising. But,
not only have advertising costs soared, but there is now also a profusion of media. Growing numbers of TV and radio stations allow
companies unprecedented levels of access to audiences which are
becoming progressively smaller and more fragmented.

Margins squeeze

In many businesses and entire sectors profit margins are being
squeezed dry. The supermarkets are engaged in a perpetual price war
with discounters entering the fray throughout Europe having already
wreaked havoc in the United States. The German discounter Aldi is
already blazing a trail throughout Europe. Discounters now have
approaching 10,000 German stores, 1,200 in the UK, 1,200 in Spain
and 600 in France. Numbers will almost certainly grow.

With supermarket own-label products making huge gains, once
strong brands are taking refuge in price cutting. In the past, price cutting was usually soon followed by a succession of small price
increases so that the original premium price was restored. This does
not appear to happen any more. Prices go down and stay there –
unless they can go lower still. In the UK, the newspaper price wars
between *The Sun* and the *Daily Mirror* brought a reduction in prices.
Even more drastic was the war between *The Times* and other broad-
sheets. One year on, prices remain low.

Performance squeeze

If margins are down and costs reduced, the performance of individuals and organisations has to be improved. Escaping from its osten-

tatious decadent image, branding has become obsessed with leveraging performance everywhere and anyhow.

Creating value

The end result is, in the phrase of our times, added-value. Companies must 'add value' throughout every single process they are involved in and then translate this into better value for consumers.

A *Financial Times* editorial on the soap wars betwen Unilever and Procter & Gamble sums it up:

> *'It does not matter how mundane the product. Consumers are more demanding than ever before – and competitors more ruthless. The manufacturer that fails to appreciate these facts will go to the wall.'*[1]

Key questions for companies in the 1990s

In the turbulent 1990s companies must continually answer a number of key questions concerning themselves and their brands. These questions are listed in Figure 3.3 overleaf.

Time competitive – how quick are they?

- Are decisions made speedily?

- Can they move heaven and earth to get something important done?

- Are they the fastest in the business at converting orders into completed deliveries?

- Are they the fastest in the business at converting ideas into products?

People competitive – have they the right people with the right training?

- Is training handled in an ad hoc manner as an occasional indulgence rather than systematically as a commercial necessity?

- Do people take responsibility for their own development?

- Is everyone trained regularly or are senior managers missed out?

- Does the organisation have a clear idea of the competencies required of its staff?

- Are manning levels higher than those of competitors?

Cost competitive – how expensive is running the business, now and tomorrow?

- Is cost control regarded as the responsibility of the finance department and no-one else?

- Is controlling costs regarded as more important than satisfying customers?

Productivity – is the organisation productive enough?

- Does the organisation have any systematic means of measuring productivity?

- How do productivity levels compare with those elsewhere in the industry?

- How is productivity going to be enhanced in the future?

Figure 3.3   Key questions

THE LANGUAGE OF BRANDS

The language of management is a potent (though sometimes impotent) pot-pourri of acronyms, bastardisations and other ad hoc combinations of words and phrases. The world of brands is, for better or worse, no exception. The key phrases are as follows:

Brand audit

Assessing the current situation among the brands managed by a particular company. Usually the prelude to producing a valuation of the brands, but a useful exercise in its own right.

Brand awareness

The percentage of consumers or potential consumers who have knowledge of or can identify a particular brand. A brilliantly conceived brand, backed by a highly expensive marketing campaign, may make little impact on the audience. Companies have, therefore, to discover how many consumers can spontaneously recognise their particular brand and how it compares to recognition of other competing brands.

Brand cannibalism

Introducing a new brand which will eat into the market for other of your own brands.

Brand equity

The financial and commercial value of the brand to the organisation which owns and utilises it. This is a simple idea but calculating it with any degree of accuracy or credibility is a complex (perhaps impossible) task. The problem is that any brand is in a constant state of flux. A pejorative adjective in a newspaper article can cause irreparable damage; the collapse of a competitor can provide an unexpected bonus.

It is also easy to confuse the asset and the value of the asset. Tim Ambler and Chris Styles of London Business School say:

'It is like the difference between a house as an asset and the financial worth of that asset. The house may have many different valuations depending on the circumstances and assumptions used for valuation, eg for sale, purchase, insurance, probate. The variations of valuation neither change the asset itself nor deny its existence.'

Brand equity, therefore, needs to be looked at in the long term rather than as an instant source of profits. Styles and Ambler define it as

'the aggregation of all accumulated attitudes in the extended minds of consumers, distribution channels and influence agents, which will enhance future profits and long-term cash flow'.

Brand extension, line extension

First comes a brand. It is a success, so the maker or provider seeks to 'extend' the brand by introducing variations of it in the same area. Examples include Silk Cut Extra Mild, Cherry Cola or Fosters Ice. Interestingly, the new extension competes against the original brand – drinkers of Fosters Ice may be previous buyers of Fosters Draught (or, ideally, drink both). Brand extension has become endemic.

Brand loyalty

A measure of the commitment or obligation felt by consumers to purchase or use a particular brand. Brand loyalty was once highly significant, now consumers are in the habit of shopping around and of changing brands with greater frequency.

Brand premium

One of the main attractions of brands is that they routinely charge a higher price. Consumers are prepared to pay a premium price for the reassurance, kudos or feeling of well-being they receive when they buy a particular brand. The challenge for companies is to know how high a price they can charge without reducing their market share.

Brand stretching

An increasingly common strategy involving applying an existing brand to a completely different business area or a new product or service – such as Virgin's forays into cola, financial services and publishing. The risk attached to brand stretching is that failure in the new field may affect the core product.

Brand switching

Moving from one brand to another. Consumers are increasingly fickle and more demanding. They are, as a result, prone to move their affiliation from one brand to another in an indiscriminate way, much to the annoyance of brand managers.

Brand value

The financial worth of a brand or a group of brands. Though there is no formula for calculating the value of a brand it is increasingly estimated and included in company accounts.

Brand vandalism

Stretching the brand irresponsibly into markets or products it is ill-matched with, causing damage to the core brand – if Moet & Chandon puts its name to a brand of cider, this would be brand vandalism.

Own-label

A product branded by the retailer selling it. Increasingly popular as own-label products mean greater profit margins for retailers. Ironically, many of the branded products they compete against are identical in all but name.

Note

[1]   'Soap and chips', *Financial Times*, 21 December 1994.

4

THE REAL TEMPTATION OF BRANDS: INTEL

INTRODUCTION

Brands are highly tempting. Even hard-headed, no-nonsense managers are impressed by the power of brands. They like the glamour, the glitz and the concept that brands make more money. They love the idea of customers who come back time and time again. They know brands work, so they want some of their own ... even if they don't need them.

Some of the toughest managers appear susceptible to pointless brand creation. The conglomerate Hanson, for example, takes up expensive television time to advertise its name. It boasts of its international successes – 'The British company that's big over there'.

> **Brands are highly tempting. Even hard-headed, no-nonsense managers are impressed by the power of brands.**

It is very impressive. But, you soon begin to wonder, why is Lord Hanson bankrolling a commercial? Do we really need to know the Hanson brand name. If we buy Ever Ready batteries are we doing so because we know the company is owned by Hanson? Awareness of the Hanson brand is, in all probability, important to only a very small percentage of the television viewers. Are institutional investors likely to be impressed by a glossy television advertisement? Obviously Hanson thinks so, but there is a suspicion that this is an unnecessary diversion from the real business of running

Hanson's companies and its myriad of successful brands. Interestingly, it is difficult to imagine BTR – the conglomerate Hanson is most readily compared to – investing its money in a similar way.

Brands are tempting. Creating Hanson as a brand might be a good idea, but there is a suspicion that the company is investing in something which is peripheral to the real business.

INTEL

Perhaps the finest example of the temptation of brands is Intel's 'Intel Inside'. There was some confusion when Intel first launched its Intel Inside campaign. The computer buff might have known that Intel made microchips found in the recesses of computers; the vast majority of computer owners and users did not. And, quite simply, they didn't really care. When buying a computer from Dell or Compaq, you don't ask who made the chips.

However, Intel wanted us to know – even though it already held over 80 per cent of the PC-chip market. Its nearest rival, Micro Devices, had 1994 sales of $700 million; against Intel's $8.4 billion in a market worth $10 billion. Intel wanted everyone to be aware of what was inside their computers doing the real work. At huge cost, the Intel Inside campaign worked. People are now aware that Intel makes chips. In 1993 Intel was voted the world's third most valuable brand by *Financial World* magazine. Valued at $17.8 billion (compared to the worth of its nearest competitor at $4.1 billion) Intel only lagged behind Marlboro and Coca-Cola. Quite an achievement.

Intel followed this campaign with one for its Pentium chip. The logic behind this was that the Pentium was the newest and most powerful PC-chip on the market. The Pentium was Intel's successor to the highly successful 266, 386 and 486 chips.

After its launch at the beginning of 1994, Intel anticipated sales of the Pentium would reach in excess of 10 million units by 1996. The campaign encouraged people to switch from 486 machines to Pentium PCs. This all sounds very laudable but, as Intel made the 486 chips, the company was waging a campaign against itself. The campaign worked – it increased awareness of the Pentium and also succeeded in annoying companies, such as Compaq, which were still putting their efforts into selling 486s. Compaq's marketing needed to find ways round the suggestion from the chip maker that the 486 was basically obsolete.

Of course, having revealed to the world that it makes the chips, Intel's troubles begin if the chips are wrong. It may be three million transistors on a minute bit of silicon, but we expect it to be perfect and, thanks to Intel's marketing, if there is a fault in the chip we now know who to blame. Forget Dell or IBM, call Intel.

'With Intel Inside you know you've got … unparalleled quality', reads an Intel advertisement. The 'unparalleled quality' boast appeared a little excessive in late-1994 when Thomas Nicely, a mathematics professor at Lynchburg College, Virginia, achieved international renown. Professor Nicely found that his three Pentium computers were making mistakes and then, in an effort to get to the bottom of the mystery, shared his discovery on the Internet. Thanks to the miracles of modern technology, a minor mathematical problem became an international incident and, thanks to Intel's advertising, people knew where the fault lay.

In December 1994, IBM announced that it was halting shipments of the affected PCs and Intel was forced to adopt a vigorous damage limitation exercise.

The fault was small – Intel calculated it would afflict the average user only once ever 27,000 years; IBM countered that some customers could encounter the fault every month. 'For a customer with 500 Pentium-based PCs, this could result in as many as 20 mistakes a day', said IBM. Coincidentally, IBM was also developing machines with its own chip:

'After years watching Intel build its brand at IBM's expense, Big Blue must have found this as emotionally satisfying as a long-suffering sugar daddy cancelling an errant mistress's credit card',

observed The Economist.[1]

Whatever the nature and regularity of the flaw, Intel clearly had set itself up. Ironically, the problem with the Pentium was far less significant than flaws found in previous chips, the only difference was that Intel had marketed the brand too successfully. Not only had five million Pentiums been manufactured, but the Pentium was backed by an $80 million marketing campaign to encourage the market to make the switch from the old (the 486) to the new (the Pentium). This came on top of the estimated $70 million spent on the Intel Inside campaigns.

Intel's disaster was not, in fact, as costly as it might have been. At the beginning of 1995 it set aside $475 million to cover the costs of replacing the flawed Pentiums. Its revenues in 1994 were $11.52 billion, up 32 per cent on the previous year. But the long-term fall-out is not yet clear.

Chip lessons

Intel's problems were largely of its own making. It created the brand and has to live with the consequences. Also, it is clearly a victim of its own success. The bigger the name, the bigger the brand, the keener competitors, onlookers, commentators and journalists are to topple it from its pedestal. Even so, Intel's Pentium disaster was not simply a story of hubris or technology gone wrong. There are some general lessons:

> **The bigger the name, the bigger the brand, the keener competitors, onlookers, commentators and journalists are to topple it from its pedestal.**

- React quickly but don't play down the problems – Intel's first reaction was that IBM's tests were 'contrived'. This may or may not have been the case, but to the casual observer it had the ring of a bitter retort rather than a considered judgement aimed at helping customers.

- You may know your business, but you don't necessarily know better. Intel president and chief executive Andy Grove struck a false note with his initial pronouncements, seeming to suggest that the controversy was caused by ignorance and media hype:

'We are quite clearly anxious to have this event behind us, but given that this has become a major event in the mass media, involving people who are not accustomed to dealing with sophisticated mathematical terms like random divides, operands and floating points, quite frankly we don't know what to do',

said Grove.[2] Don't patronise.

- Recall or come up with a solution. Initially Intel offered to replace chips for customers who could prove that their machines were needed for accurate complex computations. It was only later in December that it offered to replace processors free of charge.

'Our previous policy was to talk with users to determine whether their needs required replacement of the processor. There was a resentment to our approach – it appeared that we at Intel were arrogant, we were telling customers what was good for them. Maybe we have been thick-headed ... but we finally figured it out',

observed Andy Grove.[3] On 22 December Intel took a full-page advertisement in the *Financial Times* to apologise:

'No microprocessor is ever perfect', it said. *'What Intel continues to believe is that an extremely minor technical problem has taken on a life of its own. Although Intel firmly stands behind the quality of the current version of the Pentium processor, we recognise that many users have concerns. We want to resolve these concerns.'*

- Brands aren't a sideline or an indulgence. They have to be managed in the same way as any other part of the business. Intel appeared like a group of computer enthusiasts who had stumbled into a marketing seminar and then couldn't find a way out.

- Learn lessons. More positively, Grove has gone out of his way to stress that lessons will be learned.

'The Pentium processor divide problem has been a learning experience for Intel. In the end, I think it will strengthen the company by improving our policies and infrastructure for serving customers.' [4]

- Up the pace. 'There are the quick and there are the dead', Andy Grove is reputed to have observed. Intel has proved itself able to re-invent itself continually – the focus of its marketing, for example, has moved from selling product features in the early 1970s to direct partnership with the final customers of the company's microprocessors in the 1990s.

It would have been tempting for Intel to put itself below the parapet for a while, instead it pushed forward and, before the Pentium contoversy subsided, announced its next generation of chips, the P6.

Notes

[1] 'Intel's chip of worms?' *The Economist*, 17 December 1994.
[2] Kehoe, L., 'Article of faith challenged', *Financial Times*, 14 December 1994.
[3] Kehoe, L., 'Intel offers to replace Pentium microchips', *Financial Times*, 21 December 1994.
[4] Kehoe, L., 'Pentium charge cuts Intel profit by $475 management', *Financial Times*, 18 January 1995.

5

THE REAL POWER OF BRANDS

INTRODUCTION

Of course, the first question must be: why bother? Isn't branding simply about gimmickry? Wouldn't it be more sensible and commercially attractive to be brand-free?

Why did Intel feel the need to create a brand when it already controlled the market? The answer is that Intel wanted to create loyalty among customers before other manufacturers got a foot into the market and began to do the same. Without the Intel Inside campaign, consumers had nothing to be loyal to.

The commercial advantages of effective and consistent branding are increasingly identified and quantified, as are the disadvantages. The major benefits are:

- Increasing customer loyalty – customers can develop strong affiliations to particular brands. This enhances market share.
- Differentiation – being and seeming different from the competition is increasingly important. In hyper-competitive markets, brands offer a flexible means of differentiating products and services which may in many ways be identical.
- Pricing – such is the reassurance of quality associated with the brand that it can allow a premium price to be charged. Equally, strong brands can often undercut rivals simply because their name is better known or associated with certain characteristics.
- Brands can invent and transform markets – the development of many markets has been driven by or associated with the rise of brands.
- Defying product maturity – brands can enable products to resist

the normal cycle of product maturity.

- Creating new identities – branding previously unbranded products and services can create new commercial possibilities, partnerships and networks.

- Defeating reality – brands can allow organisations to overcome annoying obstacles of reality. The abstract world of the brand can be a bulwark against the harsh winds of day-to-day reality.

INCREASING CUSTOMER LOYALTY

Customers are not revolutionaries. They are attracted to the certainty of knowing that what they buy will be good value for money or will perform a particular task effectively. They are cautious and easily disappointed. Their loyalty is key to business success – and brands can create loyalty.

Brands provide a signpost to certainty and safety. Ideally, customers see a product and it triggers a host of positive thoughts so the product is bought. Some products, but only a small number, have reached this level (see Figure 5.1). Think of a carpet cleaning device and you think of Hoover. Think of a top quality car and you'll probably think of Rolls Royce. Similarly, a Mars bar will supply energy, Heineken will refresh distant parts of your body and Avis will always try harder.

Everyone in business has been told that success is all about enticing and retaining customers. It sounds reassuringly simple and achievable. But, in reality, words of wisdom are soon forgotten. Once companies have seduced customers they often overlook the second half of the equation. In the excitement of beating off the competition, negotiating prices, securing orders and delivering the product, managers tend to become carried away. They forget what they regard as the humdrum side of business – ensuring that the customer remains a customer.

Failure to concentrate on retaining as well as attracting customers costs businesses huge amounts of money annually. It has been estimated that the average company loses between 10 and 30 per cent of its customers every year. In constantly changing markets this is not surprising – what is surprising is the fact that few companies have any idea how many customers they have lost.

The ultimate for any brand is to become the name people use automatically to describe a particular product or service. In one case, a Filipino beer company changed its brand name to cerveza, the Spanish for beer. Inspired, but illegal (as top brewer San Miguel soon proved). Among the ultimate brands are:

Hoover: despite the fiasco of its free flights to the United States, we still 'Hoover' carpets.

Rolls Royce: the Rolls remains the epitome of ostentatious driving. If you are thinking of a luxury car you say Rolls Royce without thinking.

Xerox: 'Please Xerox this for me' was a phrase which rang through the corridors of the corporate world for many years. Now, sadly for the eponymous company, its name is less often used than the slightly duller, 'copy'. Anxious to move on, Xerox now puts an explanatory line under its name: 'The document company'.

Filofax: the filofax had actually been around for many years before it was rediscovered in the 1980s by energetic yuppies anxious to organise as many deals as possible into a single day. The phrase 'personal organiser' still resounds of filing cabinets and tedious good order, while filofax has a ring of urgency.

Figure 5.1 The ultimate brands

Only now are organisations beginning to wake up to these lost opportunities and to calculate the financial implications. Cutting down the number of customers a company loses can make a radical difference in its performance. Research in the US found that a 5 per cent decrease in the number of defecting customers led to profit increases of between 25 and 85 per cent.

Rank Xerox takes the question of retaining customers so seriously that it forms a key part of the company's bonus scheme. In the US, Domino's Pizzas estimates that a regular customer is worth more than $5,000 over ten years. A customer who receives a poor quality product or service on their first visit and as a result never returns, is losing the company thousands of dollars in potential revenue (more if you consider how many people they are liable to tell about their bad experience).

Increasingly the emphasis is on building relationships with customers to create loyalty so that they return time and time again. Creating customer loyalty can appear relatively simple. Everyone who buys a Land Rover Discovery, Defender or Range Rover receives a telephone call or a postal questionnaire asking them what they think about the product they have just bought. This is hardly earth shattering, but gives customers an opportunity to voice their opinion and makes it clear that there is more to the customer-supplier relationship than a simple purchase.

In the car market, customer loyalty has long been recognised as a vital ingredient in long-term success. Research in the US showed that a satisfied customer usually stays with the same car manufacturer for 12 years, purchasing another four cars within that time. Not surprisingly, buying a car now guarantees a steady deluge of information and sales literature from the car manufacturer as they try to ensure that you are not tempted elsewhere.

Once on the road, customer loyalty programmes can be seen at every petrol station. In the UK they are long-established. The simple purchase of petrol is not really affected by price – left to their own devices, customers would stop at the nearest petrol station and fill up. Customer loyalty programmes make it a more complex matter. The first petrol station might offer points to be used at Argos for which you have already collected ten partly filled cards; another might offer tokens (collect 12 and you get a baseball cap); and so on. The choice is endless and, peculiarly, has become part of our culture – people still talk about Green Shield stamps, treasure the football coins they collected in 1970 and drink from wine goblets (free with 25 tokens in the mid-1980s).

The logic behind nurturing customer loyalty is impossible to refute. 'In practice most companies' marketing effort is focused on getting customers with little attention paid to keeping them', says Adrian Payne of Cranfield University's School of Management and author of *The Essence of Services Marketing*.

'Research suggests that there is a high degree of correlation between customer retention and profitability. Established customers tend to buy more, are predictable and usually cost less to service than new customers. Furthermore, they tend to be less price sensitive and may provide free word-of-mouth advertising and referrals. Retaining customers also makes it difficult for competitors to enter a market or increase their share of a market.'

Professor Payne points to a ladder of customer loyalty. On the first rung, there is a prospect. They are then turned into a customer, then a client, supporter and finally, if the relationship is successful, into an advocate persuading others to become customers. Developing customers so that they travel up the ladder demands thought, long-term commitment and investment.

Customer loyalty programmes

Customer loyalty programmes cover a multitude of activities from customer magazines to vouchers and gifts. Basically, a customer loyalty programme aims to persuade a person to use a preferred vendor in order to take advantage of the benefits on offer, whether a trip to Acapulco or a price-reduction voucher for a calorie controlled can. Sceptics may mutter that there is nothing new in this. Indeed, businesses have been giving long-standing customers discounts and inducements since time immemorial. What is now different is the highly organised way in which companies are attempting to build relationships and customer loyalty.

The process can begin even before the potential user is born. Nappy manufacturers are a prime example of companies which take a long-term view. Prospective parents are bombarded with sample packs, free information and literature about what will be best for their soon to arrive son or daughter. By the time of the birth, the parents already have some degree of loyalty to a company whose product they have never actually bought. It can seem excessive, but one nappy company estimates that a sales increase of a single per cent would pay for its entire customer loyalty programme.

Miles of loyalty: the airline business

Nowhere is customer loyalty more highly thought of than in the airline business. It has become a key differentiating factor. Invented in the early 1980s, frequent flyer programmes are now well established and expanding rapidly in Europe where BA established its scheme in 1991. The beauty of the programmes is that the concept is simple and relatively cheap to administer. Programme members earn 'points' or 'miles' with every flight which can be redeemed for free tickets or upgrades to business class. Virgin's Freeway programme is a little more imaginative and offers hot-air balloon trips, flying lessons and visits to health clubs. The programmes mean an airline attracts and retains customers at a marginal cost while filling empty seats. The only downside is for the companies who actually pay for the travel – they get the bill while their employees receive the perks.

Though the idea is simple enough, frenzied competition means that airlines are continually changing rewards and rules to outdo others in the market. Early in 1994, for example, British Airways doubled the number of points available for those who took a flight before a certain date; BA and American Airlines, keen to boost the lethargic German market, offered triple points to German travellers; Scandinavian Airline Systems offered business class passengers starting from the UK a free overnight stay in a Scandinavian hotel; and Alitalia announced a similar scheme for flights from Italy to London.

This sort of feverish activity is not unusual. Clearly, frequent flyer programmes work. One survey estimated that a quarter of Europe's business air travellers decide on their carrier because of frequent flyer points. Carlson Marketing Group estimates that there are 32 million frequent flyer members in the US clocking up huge amounts of free travel. American Airlines' AAdvantage scheme claims 16 million members.

From the point of view of the airlines, frequent flyer programmes offer the treasure at the end of the marketing rainbow: information. Airlines have historically been starved of information about their customers because only 15 per cent book direct with the airlines – the vast majority use travel agents and other sources. Frequent flyer programmes give airlines priceless competitive information so they can target their marketing more accurately and really focus on particular market segments.

The use of technology

Technology means that customer loyalty programmes are becoming ever more sophisticated. When it comes to creating loyal customers, the database is king. When nappy makers introduced trainer pants to the UK they were relying on the power and accuracy of their databases to steal a march on their rivals. Procter & Gamble, Kimberly-Clark and Peaudouce each has a database which identifies families with children of potty-training age. The families were then deluged with special offers and various other inducements – Procter & Gamble's Pampers brand helped its publicity campaign along with an achievement chart ('I can poo in my potty' being the primary goal).

Databases mean that companies can target audiences more effectively. A DIY chain, for example, has a discount card which entitles holders to an annual payout – in the form of a voucher to be spent at the shop. The details of the cardholders enable the store to send out regular mailings to customers giving them advance warning of special offers and giving them an extra 5 per cent discount on certain days.

Technology also means that one customer loyalty programme tends to blend into another. Take someone travelling for business. He or she decides to fly with Swissair to boost their points. They might then transfer to Delta which has a reciprocal arrangement with Swissair. Having clocked up the maximum number of points, on arrival at their destination the manager surveys the massed ranks of car rental companies and plumps for the one with an agreement with the airline. They then drive to a hotel in an international chain which also offers discounts.

'The cycle is never ending with loyalty to one product or service being bolted on to another', says management consultant and author Tim Foster.

'The rapid expansion of customer loyalty programmes is proof that if they are well thought-out then they can have a great impact. If they are poorly constructed, the effect can be disastrous.'

Risks attached to customer loyalty programmes

Some customer loyalty programmes come dramatically unstuck. A leading airline recently withdrew from the Australian market. This left thousands of angry Australians stranded. They had faithfully collected points on the airline's frequent flyer programme and, unless they paid to fly to Hawaii, had nowhere to put the points to use. The airline's reputation has been damaged, probably beyond repair. Hoover's offer of free flights to the United States is perhaps the best known disaster of recent times, costing the company tens of millions of pounds and senior executives their jobs.

'As with any kind of promotion or marketing activity there are risks attached to customer loyalty programmes', says Tim Foster. 'They can also be expensive. Producing a glossy magazine for customers throughout the world is far from cheap. Companies have, therefore, to carefully balance potential pay-offs with the actual cost of the programme.'

In fact, putting the simple idea into practice has become increasingly complex. Customers are now more demanding and fickle than ever before. They are organised and use their lobbying power more effectively. Expectations are high, but companies are quickly realising that customers with a conscience create new markets.

Companies are now developing loyalty programmes which are directly related to the conscience of their customers. There are a plethora of products which pledge to donate money to help save the rain forests or support medical research, if you buy them. A supermarket chain, for example, gives customers vouchers which they can take to their children's schools to save up for a computer. Such loyalty building creates a situation in which all sides appear to win though, of course, the supermarket wins the most through creating a loyal customer.

Customer loyalty programmes are likely to become ever more ambitious. The potential for mutually beneficial link-ups is never ending. A credit card from General Motors would have been unthinkable a few years ago. Now, it is the tip of an expanding iceberg.

Supermarket loyalty

As with so many issues, it is in the supermarket that the real battle over customer loyalty is being fought. Retailers have the advantage that they have direct face-to-face contact with customers on a regular basis. Companies which have to make do with occasional meetings with customers have already developed sophisticated means of keeping in touch so that brand loyalty is constantly fostered. They send newsletters and pepper people with information as they approach the optimum time to purchase again. In the past, supermarkets have not had to work hard at customer loyalty. Now, with increasing competition, they are examining how to turn customers into loyal customers.

The possibilities are immense. There are a huge variety of customer loyalty building tools and techniques. Supermarkets require ones which are sympathetic to and build their core brands. The means of increasing customer loyalty must be sympathetic to the brand.

Boots the Chemist is a good example of a retailer which has been sitting on a hugely powerful brand for decades. Only now is it actively nurturing it. Early 1995, for example, saw the launch of The Boots Magazine, a quarterly publication which aims to tap into the 27 million customers who go to Boots every month. The magazine is particularly targeted towards women aged between 25 and 40 whom Boots consider core customers. The magazine aims to transfer the core values of the Boots brand to a magazine. Interestingly, though the magazine clearly comes from Boots, customers have to pay for it and it carries advertising from competitors. This demonstrates how far company magazines have developed from the glorified newsletters of the past and how their remit has shifted from propaganda to brand-building.

Boots has become more aware of its brand strength in many other ways. Its own-label products, for example, have grown substantially and now account for 43 per cent of sales. Its own-label brands are not all at the cheap end of the market. It has a range of basic products, such as shampoo, which is relatively cheaply priced; it also has its own brands which compete with well-known brands but cost slightly less; and, finally, a premium range which competes head-on with Body Shop products.

Growing brand awareness is often built around the increasing sophistication of retailing technology. Technology means that retailers can take customers forward to the past. From being monolithic and unfriendly, with their expanses of polished lino and queues at the checkouts, supermarkets are anxious to prove that they are human too. The human touch is back in fashion as supermarkets attempt to recreate close relationships between customers and retailer. The successful retail brands of the future will be those that most successfully add humanity to their brand.

Technology and the use of smart cards: In February 1995, the UK retailer Tesco made its move towards breaking barriers with the introduction of a 'loyalty card' called Clubcard. With predictable optimism, Tesco chairman Sir Ian MacLaurin said: 'Clubcard will enable us to recreate the old tradition of a shop manager knowing all the people who shop in his store.' Cynics might point out that in fact it is the computer which will know the customers. To the average checkout operator a customer is going to be as much of a stranger as ever.

The card gives people points according to how much money they spend and, every quarter, they receive money-off vouchers. There is nothing particularly new in the Tesco card, it uses smart card technology combined with an old idea. The big question must be what can and will Tesco do with the information it gathers on its customers.

This is an area which has not been fully explored by retailers. They have tended to regard customers in general terms rather than being able to pinpoint high spending groups or individuals. Someone who buys a couple of sandwiches once a week is treated the same as a family who buys all its week's groceries at the same supermarket spending £10,000 a year.

Technology provides the opportunity to find out more about customers and to direct special offers and discounts at individuals. Examples such as Tesco's Clubcard may be the start of a revolution in the use of smart cards as a means of building brand loyalty.

There are already around 1.25 billion smart cards in circulation across the world. For those suspicious of such technological wizardry which enables you to spend money even quicker than before there is nothing but bad news. Countries like Denmark, Finland, Switzerland and Taiwan are already wielding what has been labelled the 'electronic purse' and there are a host of pilot projects and experiments. Dublin airport has trialled using a multi-service smart card to pay for toll charges, parking and telephone calls.

'People often think that smart cards are too clever and too expensive. There are a lot of mistaken preconceptions', says Denise Lathom-Sharp, managing director of smart card consultants and developers Cardinal.

'People tend to associate smart cards with the financial services sector, regarding them as clever credit cards. But there is increasing awareness that smart card applications go far beyond financial services.'

Setting the pace are the French. While card fraud is on the increase elsewhere, in France losses have decreased significantly and smart card enthusiasts believe this can be largely attributed to French usage of smart cards. The French financial system is now geared towards the smart card in a way yet to be emulated elsewhere – there are an estimated 22 million smart cards in the French banking system. The popularity of smart cards in France can partly be attributed to the fact that the card's inventor is French and the technology has been championed by France's Bull among others. 'In France smart cards are making significant in-roads into the retail sector', observes ICL consultant Ian Chandler.

> *'Elsewhere retailers are suspicious that if they invest in smart cards there are no guarantees that the banks won't take a different route which will render their investment useless. For retailers it is catch 22.'*

Join the club

In building customer loyalty exclusivity is key. The Tesco card is available to all who shop at the supermarket but is invitingly entitled the Clubcard, suggesting that it is exclusive. Adding a club element to a brand can be an important vehicle to increasing customer loyalty. In Holland there is a club for cats run by Felix pet food. Over 100,000 fortunate felines are now members. As they nibble through their early morning helping of Felix they can browse through their mail – special offers, vouchers and information sent directly to them rather than to the penny-pinching owner. Cats can even recommend other cats for membership.

The club concept is one being effectively used by Microsoft which has its own client club 'Microsoft Plus'. Members pay a subscription of £29.95 and receive software, technical support, various special savings and a bi-monthly magazine, *Microsoft Plus*. It is expected that the magazine's circulation will rise to 30,000 in the UK and potentially 100,000 throughout Europe. Free of commercial advertising, *Microsoft Plus*, is targeted at real enthusiasts i.e. important customers who will buy more in the future and are likely to influence the buying decisions of others.

A survey into the effectiveness of Microsoft Plus found that members were on average 75 per cent more satisfied with the service they received from the company than non-members. 'We're now in the enviable position of having nearly 80 per cent of Microsoft Plus members willing to recommend us to others', says Microsoft End User marketing manager Andy Pickup. 'Microsoft Plus caters for those customers who are in some way the orphans of the software industry – people who rely heavily on their PC for their business or home needs and yet do not have access to a format IT department.'

Build from knowledge

While there are a myriad of ways to become closer to customers, successful brands are built on long-term knowledge and understanding of customer needs rather than isolated initiatives. Research by Coopers & Lybrand in 1993 found that customer loyalty schemes are 'not a durable substitute for a competitively deficient retail strategy'. A smart card might allow a retailer to paper over the cracks for a period, but it cannot by itself bring long-term success.

> **While there are a myriad of ways to become closer to customers, successful brands are built on long-term knowledge and understanding of customer neds rather than isolated initiatives.**

Indeed, research by the Henley Centre suggests that loyalty schemes have only marginal effects – improving customer satisfaction by between 2 and 5 per cent. Loyalty schemes are useful components of an overall brand identity, but they should not be regarded as the core element.

Six ways to create loyal customers

Loyalty has to be earned. Among the most obvious means of creating loyal customers are:

1 Measure customer retention.
2 Organise rewards and bonuses around retention.
3 Use technology to get closer to customers.

4 Communicate with customers imaginatively and regularly.

5 Allow and encourage customers to communicate with you.

6 Think of customers in the long term rather than as short-term sales.

DIFFERENTIATION – BEING AND SEEMING DIFFERENT FROM THE COMPETITION

In his influential book *Competitive Advantage*, Harvard Business School's Michael Porter contends that there are three ways by which companies can gain competitive advantage: by becoming the lowest cost producer in a given market; by being a differentiated producer (offering something extra or special to charge a premium price); or by being a focused producer (achieving dominance in a niche market). Brands play a key role in achieving all three routes to competitive advantage.

In 1881 in Atlanta, Georgia, a pharmacist called John Pemberton came up with a brain tonic. It became Coca-Cola. In 1894 Caleb Bradham in North Carolina began to sell a drink he had developed to help relieve dyspepsia. It contained pepsin and evolved into Pepsi-Cola.

You would, even if you were a reincarnation of Pemberton or Bradham, have difficulty tasting Pepsi and Coke apart. Their difference, in reality, is not concerned with the mystery of their ingredients, but their branding.

Brands play a crucial part in differentiating one company's products from another's. Shampoo, for example, is much the same. Add the word 'Silk', however, and you quickly differentiate even though you don't necessarily change the product. Similarly, if you add the word 'new' to a package it is quite likely to sell 30 per cent extra for a short period. Differentiation may be crass or subtle, but it is vitally important.

If a product or service has become indistinguishable from its rivals, it has become a commodity. A commodity (like coffee, oil or aluminium) sells chiefly on price. This happened to personal computers (PCs) in the 1980s. Previously, consumers had been wooed by the brand difference offered by IBM. This came in the form of security, confidence and quality. When companies and consumers realised that PCs were indistinguishable there was no need to pay extra for IBM's brand. Reassurance went out of the window. As a result, cheap clones knocked IBM from its lofty perch.

Within the car market, for example, it is becoming ever harder to be different. The products are often developed by two or more companies and the end results are similar. What were once extras – service warranties, safety items, luxuries such as quadraphonic sound systems – are consequently becoming more important.

Take the Volvo. If you mention Volvo you do not think of a fast sports car, but of safety and, if you want to indulge in social stereotyping, people with green wellington boots. Safety has become the product, rather than the car which is not differentiated in any other major way from others on the market. Indeed, its recent advertising concentrates on the fact that it includes child seats rather than the huge power of the engine or its ability to out-race a Porsche from traffic lights. Though it is a single differentiating factor, safety is highly persuasive.

In the 1980s the new differentiating factor was quality. However, a 1995 report *Tomorrow's Best Practice* found that quality is 'no longer an adequate differentiation' between expanding and stagnant businesses. Quality is now expected. Companies have to be quality conscious in order to survive, let alone to compete.

The assumption that better products will automatically lead to more customers no longer holds. One of the most poignant images of the recession of the early 1990s was car parks and even fields full of unsold luxury cars. At one stage Mercedes Benz had £850 million worth of unsold vehicles.

Fuel for brands

When we fill our cars with petrol, the product is the same. Indeed, we don't even see the product, but often we decide to make the purchase from a particular brand name – Esso, Texaco, Mobil or even Q Eight. As the product is the same, companies have to create attractive and persuasive brands.

The brand is not the petrol but the forecourt, the facilities (that bucket of dirty cold water); the shop (all you could possibly want to buy except for country and western cassettes); the added extras (stamps, tokens, plastic coins with pictures of footballers). Selling petrol is about everything *and petrol.*

In many product areas the actual quality differences from product-to-product have declined leaving the consumer to begin to think of the products as commodities. This is a marketing manager's nightmare. A good example of this is the petroleum market in the middle of the 1980s.

At that time consumers were influenced by location and price. Ideally, they wanted cheap petrol at the service station down the road. Companies attempted to lure them with sales promotions – they even cut back television advertising to find ever more imaginative promotions (cuddly toys, nodding dogs, cheap glasses you couldn't even give away). Few stick in the memory as well as the famous 1970 Esso promotion for the World Cup which involved the entire nation collecting plastic coins with footballers on.

BP was as guilty as any company of indulging in this tasteless free for all. Indeed, its attentions had been diverted away from marketing to more technologically demanding things like exploration. It forgot that it's no use oil pouring from the wells if there aren't any cars waiting at the petrol station.

Most significantly, BP had forgotten about the BP brand which was used and abused in a huge variety of ways throughout the organisation. In 1987, BP began to become concerned about its performance and potential loss to competitors, such as Esso which seemed to be gaining share through its Tiger symbol. It asked customers what they thought of the BP brand – the results revealed that though BP was regarded as large, reliable and professional, it was also lacking in warmth, dynamism, modernity and innovation.

In response, BP launched a new identity programme around the world with a catchy slogan 'on the move'. The programme aimed to develop the BP brand, showing the company as world class, modern, dynamic, innovative and responsive to the needs and desires of consumers. To measure the goals of advertising effectiveness and cost efficiency, the company designed an advertising productivity index which relates awareness rating to media spend with a base score of 100. In 1992, BP's score was 196 compared with 77 for Shell and 84 for Esso.

Distilling differentiation

Historically the main business of the Macallan-Glenlivet distillery was in supplying bulk amounts to blenders for well-known international brands. The Macallan brand lay neglected. Eventually the company saw that the dormant Macallan name had potential. In 1967 the company began to think about the possibilities of developing its single malt whisky. In 1970 the malt was first distilled.

Unfortunately, in this unique market, the company had to wait another ten years before actually selling the product. During the ten years, any money which could have been used for an expensive marketing campaign or launch was swallowed up in keeping the company afloat. Macallan's management sought to determine the unique qualities of its product. Two were eventually identified. First, it was the only distiller left which continued to mature all its whisky in sherry wood. This traditional method, long abandoned because of scarcity and considerable cost, gave the malt a natural deep colour and a rich full flavour. Secondly, in Speyside, which has the highest concentration of distilleries and industry experts in the world, Macallan is the top selling malt.

The first of these identifiable differentiating factors provided a problem. The distilling methods for the product inevitably made it more expensive to make than other whiskies. The solution was to produce a ten-year-old Macallan at the same price as the competition's 12-year-old malt. This avoided clashing with the whisky giant head-on.

The company then sought to identify itself in the marketplace. This was done simply by commissioning a bottle which was a quarter of an inch taller. The same approach was taken to the rest of the packaging which was highly traditional. It sought to look free of modern marketing techniques and artifice. The company recognised that it is selling tradition as well as whisky.

In its advertising, Macallan also sought to differentiate itself. The traditional whisky advertisements are dominated by scenery, tartan and barley. Macallan provided the antidote with off-beat, eccentric advertising which invited consumers to find out more rather than exhorting them to purchase a bottle on the spot. The advertisements, with their curious stories, brought a flood of reaction, and more stories like the man who bicycled every year from Wales to collect his six bottles; the burglars at a local off-licence who broke in and only stole the Macallan; the ghillie who never wore his ear flaps over his ears since the disastrous day when the laird offered him a dram of the Macallan and he failed to hear. The advertising became a dialogue – something all advertisers wish to achieve.

The Macallan whisky created its own niche through a carefully thought-through strategy of differentiation. Some of it was subtle (the advertising), some obvious (such as the bottle), but it was all constructed with the final brand and its development in mind.

The slogan

In search of difference, companies are habitual users of slogans. This is a kind of insurance policy; if your packaging or identity doesn't stick in the mind of consumers, try a catchy phrase. Slogans don't just sound good in advertisements, but can give a focus to a brand and an organisation's activities.

Ironically the means of differentiation may not differentiate at all. Author and consultant Tim Foster runs a service called Foster's Database of Slogos. A 'slogo' is 'the slogan by the logo' and includes such famous phrases as 'The world's favourite airline' (BA) or 'The natural choice' (American Express). Foster's Database ensures that a company's catchy phrase has not been used before. American Express, for example, might now be aware that 'The natural choice' is also the slogo for Budget Rent-a-Car, Emmental, ITT

Sheraton, Mobil Gas, Pulsar and Scotch Beef. (Foster's Database of Slogos 0181-763 2225)

PRICING

According to research by City University Business School, consumers pay more attention to brand names than prices when they are doing their weekly shopping. This defies traditional wisdom. When walking round supermarkets we are supposed to examine the price of every product before casting it into our trolley. However, with EPOS in place in all sizeable supermarkets, the prices are not actually displayed on the products. Instead, we have to survey the shelves for displays – this takes a little more effort so we often don't bother. Instead of prices, our minds fill with the array of brand names crowded to overflowing on the polished shelves.

Pricing is where brands meet reality. Forget the esoteric talk of lifestyles etc. the real power of brands is charging prices which make your business profitable. If brands don't have some effect on pricing, they are redundant.

Pricing is where brands meet reality. Forget the esoteric talk of lifestyles etc. The real power of brands is charging prices which make your business profitable.

Nevertheless, pricing is an area of immense confusion for brands. There is a tendency to want to be all things to all people – brands can seem to want to be cheap, affordable, high quality and luxurious. This is impossible. In reality brands can compete on price, quality or as luxury products and services. Moving from luxury to price-based competition is unhealthy but common; making the journey from price competitiveness to luxury is demanding if not impossible. Brands which vary their pricing tactics are liable to confuse their customers and themselves.

Premium pricing

If you have two children and a large dog and you want to go away for the weekend, a Porsche is not the car for you. When it comes to transporting more than two adults, the Porsche is useless (the two adults can also forget about taking very much luggage). And yet, the Porsche is a status symbol, a car for which many people are willing to pay a large amount of money. They pay a premium price for the privilege and do so because of what the Porsche stands for – conspicuous wealth, speed and glamour. The mythology of the brand, combined with the features of the product, allows Porsche to charge more than you would pay for a comfortable family saloon which has room for children, dog and luggage.

From a money-making point of view the most obvious lure of brands is that they can allow you to charge top prices. Consumers are prepared to pay more because they consider brands add value; buying a particular beer or spirit gives you membership of a certain group in society, it reassures and suggests a sense of belonging. As a result, branded products and services are often more expensive than their competitors. You pay more for a tin of Heinz beans than a supermarket's own-label tin of beans because Heinz offers the reassurance of quality, consistency, tradition and past experience. You pay for the brand.

Market research has often asked consumers what they would pay for a particular new product, unnamed, and with a trusted brand name, and it is not unusual for the latter to attract a 30 per cent price premium in the research. This is good news for everyone, apart from the consumer's wallet. The maker, wholesaler and retailer can all charge more and expect larger profit margins.

Kellogg's Corn Flakes is a good example of premium pricing and of some of the problems now facing premium products and services. If you live in Battle Creek, Michigan, the home of the corn flake you will pay more for a box of the tasty flakes of real corn than someone who lives on the other side of the Atlantic. In the US, Kellogg has steadily increased prices while distributing money-off coupons which have proved persuasive enough to retain customers. In 1993, as a result, around 60 per cent of cereal purchases were made with an average 35 per cent discount. In the UK where money-off coupons are substantially less popular, corn flakes are cheaper though Kellogg still charges a higher price than own-label competitors.

In effect, Kellogg in the US has been having it both ways – a premium priced product available to most of its customers at a reduced price. This policy worked successfully until markets began to stagnate, particularly in the US. Kellogg's response was to reduce the number of coupons available (a move also taken by its rival General Mills). This cut costs, raised profits and, more importantly, effectively raised prices for a large percentage of purchasers. The end result is that Kellogg and General Mills are losing market share to own-label and smaller competitors.

Similarly, cutting advertising budgets to fund discounts may work in the short term but is unlikely to yield long-term dividends. Without significant advertising to communicate these added values, customers will become perplexed as to why they should pay a price premium and may consider shifting their loyalty.

Brand engineering

One of the most successful premium brands in the world is Castrol, owned by Burmah Castrol. While the world lubricants market has stagnated over the last decade, Castrol increased sales at a compound annual rate of nearly 6 per cent.

Castrol's 'liquid engineering' does not come cheaply. The entire thrust of the company's marketing is to encourage motorists to look after their vehicles, to pamper them by supplying them with Castrol rather than an alternative cheaper brand. In support of the brand, Castrol sponsors rallying, Formula One Racing and the Indy Car Series in the US. Thanks to such carefully targeted brand building, Castrol has raised its share of the DIY lubricants market in the US from 5 to 15 per cent in the last decade.

Castrol is taking the premium pricing a stage further in the US with a synthetic motor oil, Syntec, aimed at enthusiasts and technical specialists. Backed by $20 million invested in its launch, the new oil sells at nearly four times the price of ordinary oils. With products like Syntec leading the way, Castrol can back them up with other products at lower prices.

In Asia, Castrol is continuing its premium pricing policy and is targeting consumers with annual incomes over $18,000 per household (at the moment this only amounts to around 60 million people but, by 2000, Castrol anticipates a market of around 300 million).

Putting a premium on paper

The beauty of premium brands is that they can be applied to virtually anything. The brand adds value – literally.

A popular route to premium pricing is to add the word 'gold' to a product. Gold continues to have strong associations with exclusivity. As a result, we have Gold Blend coffee, Kodak Gold, gold American Express cards and even radio stations like Capital Gold. The power of a single word is daunting. There is added kudos in having a gold American Express card. It looks and sounds flashy.

Indeed, the flexibility of brands and the word 'gold' is such that it can cheerfully be attached to toilet paper and a premium price charged. Andrex Gold costs around 7 per cent more than ordinary Andrex (itself up to 40 per cent more expensive than own brands). Its makers, Scott, say it is 'softer, thicker, more absorbent' thanks to an 'air-dry technique'. This is all very well, but Scott also observes that the buyer of Andrex Gold 'needs reassurance' that they are buying the best for their family. This is the crux of the matter. Forget the air-dry technique, in this case the premium price pays for reassurance. We are paying to assuage our guilt.

If toilet paper can attract a premium price, given the right marketing anything can. Some can even take the difficult route from low-cost to premium pricing. Cider, for example, was once an appallingly sweet drink drunk by 16 year olds at parties or by winos on street corners. Apart from English sherry, it was the lowest common denominator. Today, cider has been transformed to appeal to a fashion-conscious highly contemporary market. The product remains sweet but brands have transformed the drink's reputation and fortunes. From being a price-based competitor, the cheapest thing you could buy to get drunk on or take to a party, it has become an object of premium pricing.

Strong brands can undercut rivals

Strong brands can charge a premium price. But, more risky, strong brands can also use their strength to undercut competitors. This is potentially dangerous but, if it works, can revolutionise entire markets.

An excellent example of this has taken place in the personal computer market over the last decade. The increased maturity of the market led to IBM's brand strength becoming less important than the price of the actual product. One of the most stunning beneficiaries of this has been the Texan computer company Compaq. In 1994 it pushed IBM and Apple aside to become the world leader in the PC market with 9.5 per cent of the world market. Compaq has reached such heady heights chiefly because of a price cutting policy which is unprecedented in its consistency and aggressiveness. Indeed, as Compaq became market leader it cut its prices by up to 29 per cent.

Compaq's has not been an unmitigated success story. Started in 1982, the company reached sales of $2 billion in 1988. At that time, making money in the computer business was relatively easy. Then reality struck. In 1991 Compaq's profits plummeted by 71 per cent. In response, Compaq got rid of its founder. It also began to cut prices and has continued to do so ever since.

Compaq's price cutting was based on the strength of its brand name. If an unknown PC maker cuts its prices, it smacks of desperation. The consumer is likely to read disaster between the lines. If a well-known brand like Compaq does so, it seems like an opportunity. Aggressive price cutting is not something any company can or should do half-heartedly. Once you have started you are immediately sending a strong signal to the marketplace that you are a low price producer. Trying to alter this perception is challenging – similarly, it is incredibly difficult for IBM to transform itself into anything other than a premium price producer.

In June 1992, Compaq launched a range of PCs which cost a third less than their predecessors. It has since cut prices at an annual rate of 30 per cent. The economics of this are simple. Compaq accepts that its profit margin is decimated – down from 43 to 27 per cent (which isn't bad by most standards). At the same time, Compaq's net profits have increased massively – first quarter profits for 1994 were $213 million, more than double the previous year's figures.

The only disadvantage is that such success revolves around constantly cutting prices and increasing the volume of goods produced, as well as making constant progress in efficiency and productivity. Compaq's statistics are impressive, to say the very least. Compaq's combined labour and overhead costs per computer have fallen by 75 per cent over two years; labour now accounts for as little as 2 per cent of its products' total costs. Astonishingly, each of Compaq's 10,500 employees accounts for an average of $716,000 in sales last year – up from $305,000 in 1991.

However, there is a limit – no matter what management consultants might say. Compaq is now looking for other areas where it can repeat the process. The crucial point is that having reshaped the market and the way people perceive the Compaq brand it simply has to make similar inroads into other areas to survive and build for the future.

As retailers are increasingly discovering, discounting is a dangerous business. In 1993 the retailing group Budgens enthusiastically adopted discounting with its 'Penny Market' format. At the beginning of 1995 it announced a drastic reduction in profits and abandoned the discounting formula. The idea originated when the German retailer Rewe took a 29.4 per cent stake in Budgens. Rewe has 1,800 Penny Market stores in Europe and believed it was a formula which would succeed elsewhere. It expressed disquiet at Budgen's withdrawal and suggested that too little time had been committed to making it work.

BRANDS CAN INVENT AND TRANSFORM MARKETS

In 1971, Tom Farmer opened the first Kwik-Fit automotive repair and parts centre. Today, there are over 600 centres in the UK, Holland, Belgium, France and Ireland.

Before Kwik-Fit came into existence, the market for quick basic repairs to exhausts existed but was inadequately catered for. Garages were unreliable and slow. Bills didn't match quoted prices and many were uninterested in small jobs like changing exhausts.

What marks Kwik-Fit apart is that it has used its brand to develop its business. What Kwik-Fit actually does is not technologically advanced, it is usually a fairly simple mechanical exercise. An exhaust is a commodity to which it brings unparalleled professionalism.

> *'Kwik-Fit's policy is to give customers first-class value for money, supplying high quality components backed by reliable guarantees. Above all, Kwik-Fit gives service; fast, courteous and professional, and always strives for 100 per cent customer satisfaction. At Kwik-Fit, this is no mere slogan; it is a constant goal.'*

In the 1970s, the Swiss watch industry was in a rut. Faced with increased competition from the Far East future prospects looked grimly predictable. Then along came Swatch, colourful, fashion-conscious, reliable, reasonably priced. The Swatch watches turned the Swiss industry upside down. Market share was 15 per cent in the 1970s; now it is over 50 per cent.

Sitting comfortably: the airline business

Times have changed for the business traveller on the world's airlines. In the past, a quickly arranged curtain divided them from the Economy passengers and a free drink was often the only obvious benefit of being in Business Class. And then the airlines discovered branding.

Leading the way was BA which set out to become the business

traveller's favourite brand, as well as 'the world's favourite airline'. The creation of a business class brand was the job of Mike Batt, then head of central marketing at BA and later marketing director until 1995.

> *'Business Class didn't exist prior to 1981, but it has grown enormously, attracting passengers from both First Class and Economy. Now our biggest single problem is providing enough seats for our business travellers',*

he said after the launch.

The problem identified by BA was that the company was basically production led. Its products were sometimes well designed but they tended to be designed round the operational needs of the airline rather than the passengers. Batt, formerly with Mars, was keen to bring the expertise of consumer goods companies to BA: 'Consumer goods companies really understand the psychology behind their products.'

Previously, competition had been based on price (as the bitter price wars of the 1970s testify) and service was a peripheral issue. The 1980s changed all that and it became a quality elastic rather than a price elastic market. In 1988, BA launched its Club World and Club Europe brands aimed specifically at business travellers. The creation of the two brands cost the airline in excess of £20 million. Club World offered passengers more leg room and a reclining 'contour-shaped' seat as well as better food and service. Club Europe recognised that the product should go beyond service in the air, offering such things as 'valet parking' for travellers to Paris and Amsterdam.

The changes, BA decided, were necessary because while consumer demands had become much more sophisticated, the airline had stood still. It recognised that Business Class passengers were used to things revolving around them rather than having their mealtimes dictated by the video to be shown.

Essential to the brand's reshaping of the market was its advertising. Traditionally airline advertising is all about seats and leg room. There was some disquiet at BA when it was decided that the new seat wasn't going to be mentioned in the advertising. Indeed, the advertisements focused instead on business people succeeding – the message, travelling with us will bring business success; rather than travel with us and you'll sit in a comfortable seat for a few hours. 'Before it was just an aeroplane. It came to mean a style of travel', says BA.

Hamish Taylor, general manager of brands at BA, has explained the revolution:

> *'If you look back to 1984 we had a re-launch of what used to be known as Super Club and what we did was tell everybody about our fantastic new seat, the biggest seat ever. Everything we did focused on that seat. Now, if you think about that, what was happening was not about the customers, and what he or she wanted from British Airways, but about this phenomenal seat, which, let's face it, was easily copied by our competitors. And of course that's precisely what they did. Very quickly we found we were losing our advantage. What we should have been doing, and have done since, was looking at the benefit to our customers. That's what we had to market, not the product itself.'*

More recently, BA has re-launched Club Europe complete with a new broader seat, telephone check-in, valet parking and better service. 'It's branding', says Taylor, 'that asks one question. Have I put it in terms that my customer understands?'¹

Creating new markets

Brands shape the development of markets. But they do not stop there. They can create entirely new market segments within an established product category. This has happened in recent years with low-calorie or low-fat versions of a huge number of food and drink products.

New brands can succeed, but

> **New brands can succeed, but they have to work extremely hard to do so. They must be differentiated and be backed by appropriate and well-financed marketing campaigns.**

they have to work extremely hard to do so. They must be differentiated and be backed by appropriate and well-financed marketing campaigns.

Child prodigies: young brands which have made it

The pantheon of brand greats is not easily entered. Many aspire to become household names, few succeed for any length of time. Cults and teenage fads may temporarily propel a brand to national attention, but this is unlikely to last long. The brand prodigies of recent years which are already proving their staying power include:

- **Mr Kipling:** made by television advertising rather than the dull packaging, Mr Kipling is automatically associated with apple pies (even if he now chooses to inject them with custard). The entire brand image attempts to take you back to a halcyon period when cricket was played on village greens and summer lasted all year long. Even the choice of Kipling is a far from subtle reminder of the only other Kipling you have ever heard of – Rudyard.

- **Gold Blend:** one of the great brands of the 1980s. It bears out the traditional wisdom of using the word 'gold' (meaning: exclusive; premium price to match). The Gold Blend television advertising campaign became an unlikely success story as viewers followed the plot involving two highly attractive coffee drinkers. 'Will they, won't they?' asked an entranced nation before promptly forgetting as soon as they had, or hadn't. The advertising became a novel, setting an unhealthy publishing trend.

- **Club 18–30:** everything you ever wanted a holiday to be when you were 18. A brilliant example of niche marketing, at one extreme Saga Holidays, at the other Club 18–30 with its promise of frenzied night life, sun, sea, sangria and sex, not necessarily in that order. The title 'club' is in itself a smart idea, it encourages a sense of belonging and suggests exclusive benefits. Clearly those under 18 and many over 30 would like to be members. Indeed, the company now calls itself simply 'Club' and recent advertisements have dispensed with any promise of sun, sea and sangria.

- **Manchester United:** soccer clubs never used to be brands. Now, they are listed on the Stock Market and behave like real companies. Manchester United stands out as the football brand. Its success is such that its dedicated supporters now include around 50 per cent of all children under ten. It has been heavily criticised for behaving as any good brand should. It now changes its strip more regularly than ever before in pursuit of brand extension and its club superstore is a retailing success story.

DEFYING PRODUCT MATURITY

Companies come and go. Indeed, they are disappearing at a far faster rate than ever before. Organisations have always experienced the ebb and flow of success and failure. They have always been prone to the cyclical sweeps of economics. Today, however, the force and speed of change means that it is becoming increasingly more difficult for organisations to hold their own, let alone prosper. Between 1955 and 1980 only 238 companies fell out of the *Fortune 500* rankings. Between 1985 and 1990, however, 143 dropped out. From the 12 companies which made up the Dow-Jones Industrial index in 1900, a single one (General Electric) remains an industrial giant. Companies are no longer reassuring presences, permanent fixtures in our towns and cities offering jobs for life and constantly sustained growth. Instead, they are fragile, impermanent and far from reassuring.

But, while companies can sink without trace, a number of brands have gone on and on:

- **Bird's Custard powder:** it is difficult to imagine why consumers need custard powder when you can now buy it in cans and cartons. But, they do.

- **Heinz soup:** the star in the firmament is tomato soup. Parallels could perhaps be drawn with Lucozade: the unwell also consume tomato soup – but Heinz has resisted the temptation to turn its brand into a sportsman's drink.

- **Kellogg's Corn Flakes:** name another brand of cornflakes? The beauty of cornflakes is that it is also a brand which has no gimmick to fall back on. Other Kellogg's brands are bolstered by cartoon characters (Tony the Tiger is a hardy perennial who has been munching his way through Frosties for many years) and Rice Krispies come complete with cartoon characters (pixie-like figures with incredible appetites whose names are now a catchphrase 'snap, crackle and pop').

- **Johnson's baby lotion:** generations of babies have been brought into the world to be coated in generous amounts of this lotion. It has become indispensable and steadfastly refuses to be beaten by incursions into its market.

- **Bisto:** the ultimate, indeed the only, gravy. In an era when the Sunday roast is increasingly a pizza, it seems strange that Bisto remains stacked high on the supermarket shelves. Unperturbed by the array of casserole mixes and sauces, Bisto remains the name for gravy.

There are many others which appear touched by the brand equivalent of immortality. They appear to be impervious to the conventional wisdom of markets maturing and then declining. They defy the ageing process and, even more strangely, some defy progress – who would have thought that Gillette would still be pronouncing it was 'the best a man can get' when electric shavers have been around for decades?

Part of the secret is to find a small but lucrative market (though these are often larger than you would think). A good example of how to defy the ageing process, up to a point at least, comes from Reckitt and Colman. In 1994, the company announced that it was to sell its highly successful mustard business after 180 years under family control. The company's success had been built round success in small uncompetitive niches – Brasso, Windolene and Harpic were all Reckitt brands. The problem was that what had previously been money-earning niches were increasingly subject to competition.

Brand rejuvenation

Some brands find that they are reincarnated after a period in the wilderness. The 1990s, for example, have seen a preoccupation with the seventies. A number of products which had either disappeared or terminally declined have enjoyed a spirited, though probably short-lived, resurgence:

- **Old Jamaica chocolate:** re-launched by Cadbury in the 1990s. The company claimed that its return was attributable to popular demand. For some reason the nation remains mysteriously sentimental about this particular rum and raisin chocolate bar. There is, however, little demand for the original advertising which featured a pirate and the slogan 'Don't 'ee knock it all back at once'.

- **Bird's Angel Delight:** re-launched with a £600,000 advertising campaign in 1993 targeted at 'thirty-something mothers'. Angel Delight never actually went away, it just seemed as if it did. For consumers its image remained firmly rooted in the 1970s when an Angel Delight was a treat. It is unlikely that anyone who experienced Angel Delight in the 1970s will now be able to say the name without attaching the prefix 'Bird's'. The pedantic will also be aware that it really should be called Kraft General Foods' Angel Delight. This, however, lacks the necessary air of nostalgia.

- **Brylcreem:** forever associated with 'traditional' barber shops with their red and white signs, uncomfortable chairs, chatty barbers and dusty displays of contraceptives and combs. Fashionable once again after a lengthy period when the Brylcreem bounce was reduced to a limp curl. However, the youthful penchant for hair gel is likely to soon disappear leaving Brylcreem as a grooming aid for the slicked-back and nostalgic.

- **British Home Stores:** converted into the more fashion-conscious BHS. British Home Stores always had a curiously dated ring to it, even when it was just invented. BHS, on the contrary, is all about a memorable corporate identity (all pastel colours and designer swirls), cheerier stores and clothes which go beyond the steady reliability of anoraks.

- **Guinness:** the old man's drink of the 1970s revived in the 1980s to appeal to a younger market. At one time Guinness seemed destined for a life alongside Mackeson (something drunk by pregnant women and ailing hospital patients) and other stouts long since past their drink-by date. Strangely, and probably perplexingly to Guinness, stouts are now back in fashion. Guinness even has competitors, Beamish (actually brewed in Ireland) and Murphy's.

- **Lucozade:** the biggest rejuvenation of all. Lucozade had one of the strongest brand names around. Unfortunately its associations were very clear – people drank it when they were ill and on no other occasion. SmithKline Beecham took consumer appreciation of Lucozade as an energy-giving drink to reinvent it as a drink to be consumed at any time you need energy. It is brilliantly simple (obvious in retrospect) but commercially dangerous. After all, Lucozade was one of the country's steadiest sellers. The tall bottles with their curious orangey-coloured wrapping were always purchased in times of illness. Sales were reliable. By reinventing the brand, SmithKline Beecham risked disrupting this steady market. Luckily for them, it worked. The world now has Lucozade Light and a number of other variations.

CREATING NEW IDENTITIES

The business world is increasingly fascinated and driven by networks. These come in all shapes and sizes. A conglomerate is a network pulled together by the identity of the centre. Brands can pull such networks together and be used to create entirely new identities.

A good example of this is the branding of places. Cities, regions and entire countries are now being transformed into brands. Open a magazine and you are assaulted by advertisements proclaiming the business benefits of relocating your entire company to a particular town or region. 'When Gio Benedetti came to Irvine he had nothing. He left with £13 million', trumpets the advertisement for Irvine, a town on the Ayrshire coast of Scotland keen to make multi-millionaires of anyone who will listen. The Port of Virginia has a logo and a slogan 'One stop America and the World'. Its advertisement even tells you how deep the water is and has a helpful map with lines emanating from somewhere in Virginia and heading to everywhere you could possibly dream of. Curiously many of these lines head inland – difficult in a ship.

Branding creates identity for places which have either lost their identity or never had one in the first place. Once Birmingham would have been associated with engineering. Now, it is 'Europe's meeting place' and is marketed by the Birmingham Marketing Partnership, a coalition of public and private sector organisations.

The Association of South East Asian Nations (ASEAN) proclaims the virtues and beauties of Thailand, Singapore and a number of other countries. The emphasis is not on culture, but on shopping: 'Browse round street bazaars, shop in supreme comfort in the many modern shopping malls or drop in at the open-air night markets. There's bound to be something which will catch your eye.'

Countries are also brandable. Indeed, flags have provided a national identity for centuries and they remain under-used, except for the Swiss flag which is widely used by Swiss companies. Other countries take a variety of approaches. 'It's for real' says the advertisement for the Maldives; Taiwan has the slightly tortured slogan 'It's very well made in Taiwan'; Portugal has the highly geographical 'Where Europe meets the Atlantic' – the brainchild of design guru Wally Olins. Spain has milked the work of Joan Miro; this is not necessarily a bad thing as his work is very Spanish in appearance, bright, instantly recognisable and transferable to many different media.

The trick is to discover your differentiating factor and then come up with a snappy slogan, campaign and image. New Zealand now uses the fern as a national symbol. This has many advantages. It can be used on virtually everything (from wine to kiwi fruits) and is already used by the country's world famous rugby team. Such a national brand is by its very nature highly general, it is a gentle reminder rather than a persuasive piece of salesmanship.

DEFEATING REALITY

The Jaguar is the epitome of the high performance British car. It is a classic. Inspector Morse couldn't drive anything else – reliable, stylish and British. As the British see a new Jaguar XJ6 disappear into the distance they may feel a sense of national pride. There can't be much wrong with a country which can put walnut trees, cowhide and metal to such creative use. Of course, they are allowing brand sentiment to overtake reality. Jaguar is owned by Ford and has been since 1989. The next Jaguar model may look quintessentially British, but will have a Ford engine and, even more ashamedly, may have been made in Lorrain, Ohio rather than Coventry, West Midlands.

The Jaguar is just one example of a basic truth which lies behind brands: brands decorate, embellish and re-invent reality. They are abstract and elusive money generating vehicles.

There is an air of unreality about the world of brands. Think of cola. Given a range of colas to drink would you be able to identify which was Pepsi and which Classic Cola or Virgin Cola. In all probability you would not.

> **To a large degree the real power of brands lies in the abstract nature of what they contain, involve and evoke.**

Brands shape markets, invent markets, differentiate products and a host of other value adding activities. But, in the end, their commercial power often rests in their very elusiveness, their abstract quality which inexplicably lures consumers. To a large degree the real power of brands lies in the abstract nature of what they contain, involve and evoke.

Note

[1] Quoted in 'Brand wars', *Business Life*, November 1994.

6

FROM MARLBORO FRIDAY TO DIAPER TUESDAY

MARLBORO FRIDAY

On 2 April 1993, the US tobacco giant Philip Morris cut the price of its branded cigarettes, including Marlboro, by 25 per cent. A day earlier, people might have thought the company was joking, but this was deadly serious. Just over a year later, on 19 June 1994, Michael Miles, the man who made the decision, resigned as chairman and chief executive of Philip Morris. The story behind what has become known as Marlboro Friday resounds with many of the vital questions which lie at the heart of branding and brand management in the modern business.

Marlboro is more than a brand. It is an international product, name and image known the world over. Its distinctive red and white colours and its advertising featuring romantic images of the classic American cowboy are universal. Yet, even icons are now facing intensifying competition and competing brands which have little respect for their venerable age and status.

Marlboro and others in the Philip Morris range had suffered from long-term loss of market share to generic (unbranded) cigarettes. (It is worth remembering that Philip Morris also produces the cheaper cigarettes which were undermining Marlboro but that the profit margins are understandably smaller.) Before Marlboro Friday, the unbranded cigarettes had claimed almost 40 per cent of the US market. Selling at half the price of Marlboro, the cheaper competitors along with RJR Nabisco's Camel brand, had sliced Marlboro's

US market share from nearly 30 per cent to just over 22 per cent. Michael Miles decided that something needed to be done.

Miles has been described as 'aloof and uncommunicative'. He is also a non-smoker and his experience was previously on the food side of Philip Morris's massive business empire in which 1993 sales totalled $61 billion. His food-based background, legend would have it, meant that Miles lacked real enthusiasm for the brand and understanding as to the business and what Marlboro stands for. With market share falling the normal solution would have been an advertising blitz or a small price cut, perhaps both. This might have prodded Marlboro's market share in the right direction.

Miles's solution was more dramatic and unexpected: a massive price cut. Cutting the price of the world's leading cigarette by a fifth to increase flagging market share was a very high-risk gamble indeed. To many commentators, observers and analysts it was a strategy driven by panic rather than by long-term considerations.

Longer-term implications

As well as making cigarettes cheaper, Marlboro Friday had other wider ranging implications. In one fell swoop it brought to an end the romantic veneration of brands which had evolved during the 1980s. Instead of secure money making machines, brands were suddenly unclothed as fallible, potential victims no matter what their size. There was an outbreak of realism – during the 1980s brands had grown largely, in many cases, due to premium pricing, fuelled by annual price increases, often up to 15 per cent. The succession of price increases had, in many markets, driven customers into the hands of competitors, hence the growth in own-label goods.

Marlboro Friday marked a new, and none too welcoming, dawn. The stock markets responded with disbelief, as they often do when caught totally unprepared. Philip Morris's shares plummeted 23 per cent in one day. (In a final insult to Michael Miles, they rose immediately after his departure.)

Miles's strategy was basically straightforward. He recognised that the company could not continue to charge a high premium price for the Marlboro brand – one which was clearly regarded by many consumers as being excessive. Perhaps with an eye to what Compaq had done in PCs, he sought to reduce prices and utilise the immense strength of the brand to drive up market share.

In fact, Miles's strategy worked. Since Marlboro Friday, Philip Morris shares have largely recovered and the company has grown its total share of the US tobacco market from 42 per cent to 46 per cent, with Marlboro alone growing from 22 per cent to 27 per cent. In July 1994 Philip Morris was able to report a 17.6 per cent surge in after-tax profits to $1.23 billion in its second quarter alone – more significant was the fact that this was the first increase in profits recorded since Marlboro Friday. Sales were up; by nearly 22 per cent in the US giving Morris 46.6 per cent market share (up 5 per cent) while Marlboro reached a record 28.5 per cent (up 6.5 per cent).

Final outcome

What eventually finished Miles's career with Philip Morris was his plan to separate the company's two core businesses: tobacco and food and drinks (including Maxwell House, Kraft and Miller beer). This met with opposition from former chairman, Hamish Maxwell, who had masterminded the company's diversification in the 1980s through eye-catching buys such as General Foods, Kraft and Jacobs Suchard.

Again Miles's logic was clear. Maxwell had built up the food side of the company's business in the 1980s when it seemed that tobacco was likely to be a declining and potentially troublesome business to be in. The strategy worked to the extent that the food side of Philip Morris accounted for almost half of its turnover by 1993, though it was far less profitable than tobacco. Miles had actually become part of Morris when it took over Kraft where he was chairman and chief executive. Experienced in the foods business, he was keen to divide the two empires – he was also reacting to the intense anti-smoking lobby in the US and the threat of litigation.

After a six-hour board meeting, Miles's plan was rejected. His position made untenable he left weeks later, to be replaced by two smokers from the tobacco side of Philip Morris's business.

DIAPER TUESDAY

The importance of Marlboro Friday is that many of the issues it raises are applicable elsewhere in the world of brands. In November 1994, for example, Procter & Gamble announced that it was reducing the price in America of its Luvs disposable nappies by 11 per cent. At the same time, the cost of raw materials was increasing massively – pulp prices had gone up by 80 per cent and were continuing to rise speedily. One estimate put P&G's consumption of pulp at 700,000 to 800,000 tonnes a year, giving it extra costs of around $200 million in the US alone.

So, why increase the price? There are clear comparisons with Marlboro Friday (indeed one article mentioned the phrase 'Diaper Tuesday', fortunately it has not been mentioned since). P&G's price cut aimed to hit back at cheaper, own-label competitors. It did so in a fiercely competitive market. US nappy prices fell by around 20 per cent between 1992 and 1994 as P&G, Kimberly-Clark (producers of Huggies) and own and private labels fought it out.

Such moves have a knock-on effect. P&G cut the price of Luvs, and then had also to reduce the price of its premium brand, Pampers, by 2 per cent – if it hadn't Pampers would have begun to look overly expensive. The repercussions were also felt in P&G's other businesses; it increased the price of its paper-based products (toilet tissues, facial tissues and paper towels) and also set about a substantial reorganisation (closing 30 plants and shedding 13,000 jobs).

Compare this with the halcyon days of the 1980s when raw materials were cheap, demand was high and prices could be pushed up with apparent abandon – a situation which applied to nappies and cigarettes.

LESSONS FROM FRIDAY

The following lessons can be learned from the experiences of Philip Morris leading up to and subsequent to Marlboro Friday.

- To achieve long-term goals, watch short-term tactics: the first lesson must be that to pursue a long-term strategy, you have to have supreme confidence that you can carry the organisation and its top managers with you. To succeed in the long term you have to have mastered short-term politics and machinations. While Michael Miles had a rational long-term strategy, he clearly did not have the full support of his colleagues. He is notoriously uncommunicative – refusing to give interviews or talk to important analysts. If you are attempting to force through such important changes you have to communicate continually with everyone.

- Don't price yourself out of the market: a brand premium should never be so high that it leads to loss of market share. A series of price increases in the 1980s left Marlboro bearing too heavy a price tag. From a pricing point of view, Marlboro now faces the hardest task. Already it has started to edge up its price. Only time will tell whether it will be able to return to its previous premium pricing policy while retaining market share.

- Don't eliminate all your margins: cutting prices necessarily reduces profit margins, unless savings can be made. There is the temptation to continue to cut prices as competitors cut theirs in the false belief that short-term sales will eventually turn into long-term profits – the end result will be that margins are wiped out altogether.

Further parallels can be made with the UK crisp industry. During the 1980s and the early 1990s, supermarkets enjoyed unfettered growth in food volumes. Then the growth slowed. Anxious to get things moving, the supermarkets cut prices. In some areas they continued to cut prices. In crisps, margins were wiped out as the price of a six-pack fell from around 85 pence to 29 pence. Reflecting on 1994, Malcolm Jones, managing director of Bensons Crisps, observed:

'We built our crisp volume by 18 per cent last year but the value by only 9.5 per cent. At that rate you become busy fools.'

In such a climate the next step is for companies to abandon the lower end of the market and seek out the world of premium pricing. Already, UB Snackfoods has targeted the premium end of the market with brands like Phileas Fogg and McCoy's. The question is how long will it be before the premium end of the market becomes crowded and prices fall in a similarly dramatic fashion?

7

HOW VALUABLE ARE BRANDS?

INTRODUCTION

People like rankings. Newspapers and magazines also like rankings because they fill space with a minimum amount of effort and provoke debate. Who is the most valuable player in the Super Bowl? If you had £10 million which footballers would you buy? What item is fashionable and which passé? Who is the richest person in the world? Which is the best business school?

Brands are also part of this populist phenomenon. Every year the magazine *Financial World* publishes a list of the world's top brands, measured by value. No doubt, every year company executives stand nervously by their fax machines or telephones waiting to be told where their organisation now stands in the glorious multi-billion dollar world of brands. The world's current top brand is Coca-Cola (worth a little under $36 billion), followed by Marlboro at $33 billion and apparently relatively unscathed by Marlboro Friday; Nescafé at $12 billion

> **The world's current top brand is Coca-Cola (worth a little under $36 billion), followed by Marlboro at $33 billion, Nescafé at $12 billion and Kodak and Microsoft each at a relatively paltry $10 billion.**

and Kodak and Microsoft each at a relatively paltry $10 billion.

According to *Financial World* up and coming brands include Timberland (robust and expensive boots), Philips (durable, but still one to watch), Tupperware (astonishingly) and Matchbox (curiously). On the way down are the likes of Max Factor, Wilkinson

Sword, Michelin, Pirelli and Siemens, though there is a nagging suspicion that these brands have been on the way out for a number of years and are still doing very nicely.

Of course, all this is highly entertaining, unless you are employed by one of the companies on the fast route to brand extinction, but does it actually mean anything? Can a realistic value be attached to brands and, if so, why stop there? After all, a company's intangible assets also include things like the skills and knowledge of its workforce. With the growth in knowledge-based businesses isn't valuing human assets more important? Perhaps this is true but the behaviour of knowledge workers is often more irrational than that of brands.

IN SEARCH OF VALUE

Brands are valuable. In one instance, reported by Richard Koch of OC&C, American Motors, a weak brand, tested a car without a brand, and consumers said they would pay around $10,000 for it. The researchers then called the car Renault Premier and the average price went up to $13,000. Then Chrysler bought American Motors, and the car was actually sold as the Chrysler Eagle Premier for around $13,000. It could, therefore, be argued that the Chrysler brand was worth $3,000 each time a car was sold.

'If this business were to be split up, I would be glad to take the brands, trademarks and goodwill and you could have all the bricks and mortar – and I would fare better than you',

John Stuart, former chairman of the Quaker Oats Company is reputed to have observed.

When a consumer buys Marlboro cigarettes or Kellogg's Corn Flakes they pay extra because of the brand. Indeed, in research on consumers' preferences for cornflakes, consumers' approval ratings went from 47 to 59 per cent once it was revealed that the product was actually Kellogg's Corn Flakes. This is a truism which has been accepted for many years.

'A brand owns a little piece of memory in the mind of the consumer with a distinctive meaning', says H. David Hennessey of Babson College in the US.

'It is a promise to the consumer to repeat that feeling or fulfil that image if he or she makes a purchase. We all immediately have this feeling or image when we hear the names of common brands such as Rolex, Marlboro, Coca-Cola, Kodak, Club-Med or Heineken. Hopefully the image or feeling is positive and will favourably influence the consumer on their next purchase.'

This little piece of real estate in the memory of consumers is one of a company's most important assets. In the past, however, the assumption has been that brands are valuable, but only in the nebulous terms of goodwill, reassurance and making customers feel good. Putting a monetary value on this feeling was presumed to be beside the point, impossible or pure folly. In the 1980s this all changed.

Assuming a monetary value

During the last decade companies woke up to the fact that if brands have a value then this value could perhaps be calculated in financial terms and, if this could be achieved, it could be included on the company's balance sheets and used to raise the price when an unwelcome (or even a welcome) predator appeared. This change meant that companies suddenly found themselves sitting on huge assets which had been there all the time but had previously been taken as worthless. This is the business equivalent of discovering that you own a goldmine.

'Although accountants have always felt much more comfortable when dealing with assets they can touch, there is now widespread acceptance that brands and other intangibles are the major assets of an increasing number of companies. Recent acquisitions, together with the high market capitalisation of listed branded

goods companies, indicate the magnitude of these "hidden" assets',

Michael Birkin, chief executive of consultants Interbrand, has observed.[1]

In putting a value on brands Interbrand has led the way. In 1988 it devised a method of brand valuation for Rank Hovis McDougall. RHM attempted to use the strength of its brands as a takeover defence. Indeed, it stated:

> *'Rank Hovis McDougall owns a number of strong brands, many of which are market leaders, which are valuable in their own right, but which the stock market tends consistently to under-value.'*

Rank Hovis McDougall eventually lost its battle, but set the ball rolling. Suddenly massive offers were pouring in for portfolios of brands. In a few months in 1988, almost $50 billion was paid for brand portfolios, including Kohlberg Karvis Roberts' $25 billion takeover of RJR Nabisco and Nestlé's $4.5 billion acquisition of Rowntree (a figure representing 26 times earnings). Instead of being decorative adornments of no intrinsic value, brands became the family silver and, with prices seemingly inflated, companies proved more than willing to sell off the silverware.

FINDING THE PRICE

The sudden acquisitive rush did not mean that the whole process of valuing brands suddenly became straightforward. Indeed, though a variety of valuation approaches emerged in the 1980s, controversy still lingers over the best method of calculating the value of a brand.

The subject of how brands are valued became highly controversial when former City analyst Terry Smith published *Accounting for Growth* in 1992. This book exposed some of the fatal flaws in attaching a value to brands and companies' interpretations of how best to do it. Smith pointed out that Grand Metropolitan's valuation of its brands (including Smirnoff and Burger King) added a massive £2.5 billion to its balance sheet – almost two-thirds of the company's assets. Similarly, over 80 per cent of Reckitt and Colman's net assets were found to relate to the value of brands acquired when it took over Boyle-Midway, a US household products group.

> 'Any system of brand evaluation should have the following attributes: it should be credible and objective, versatile and cost effective; it must be consistently applied and verifiable; and it should be relevant to the requirements of the user',

says Michael Birkin.

The Interbrand method of assessment involves a detailed assessment based on seven key elements of brand strengths:

- Leadership (dominance of market or market share).
- Stability (age and how well established).
- Market (stable or, like high-tech goods, valuable).
- Geographic spread (international brands are seen as more valuable).
- Trend (long-term trends in the brand's performance).
- Support (quality and type of marketing support).
- Protection (strength and breadth of legal protection through trademarks etc.).

The brand is scored in each of these categories against the maximum score achieved by a notional ideal brand. The trouble is finding the right weight for the seven factors and the result is inevitably open to debate. Freezing a brand at any moment in time is bound to be contentious.

'There is no direct link between the amount that has been spent on a brand in the past and its current value', says Birkin. Similarly, estimating future profits or cash flow is a highly problematic activity in any area.

Generally, to value a brand accountants compare a company's gross profits with those of a competing company or product which isn't branded. The difference between the two figures is then multiplied. The actual figure by which the difference can be multiplied may vary between 9 and 20. This depends on the strength of the brand, its position in the market and the future prospects for sales.

Until there is a universally accepted method and formula, arguments will continue. Indeed, at the moment, the process of valuing brands may be more useful than the outcome.

There are still many people who have reservations about brand valuation. The objections are many and varied. Can the brand be separated effectively from the rest of the business? Can an objective figure be extracted from subjective judgements about marketing issues? What use is a figure which can be undermined the next day by a realignment of budgets?

Indeed, valuation can never be taken as anything other than a snapshot and, at the moment, a fairly fuzzy one at that. Business history is littered with the wrecks of valuable widely admired brands which have fallen from grace. The IBM brand was ranked third in the world in 1993 and in the 1994 league tables was rated as having a negative value.

Note

' Birkin, Michael, 'How to get a grip on the great untouchables', *Financial Director*, October 1993.

8

GLOBAL AND LOCAL: BIG IN SPAIN; BIG IN SEVILLE

In the not so distant past, brands were generally, though not exclusively, national in character. The needs and tastes of consumers were conveniently assumed to correlate with borders. So, the British had the steady reliable Morris Minor, Germans had the VW Beetle and France Citroën's idiosyncratic classic the Deux Cheveaux. Today, brands and businesses know no borders. Products are no longer quintessentially German or Spanish; they may be European but are more likely to have no fixed place of birth.

GLOBAL BRANDS

The rise of globalisation has been one of the most striking trends in the business world of the 1990s. Brands have, to a large extent, led the way. Their flexibility and increasingly international nature mean that it has been automatically assumed in many quarters that particular brands are ripe for a global approach.

Many are. To prove the point, any major international sporting event will feature an array of global brands whether they are Mars, Coke, whiskies or cigarettes. Brands travel well and global brands have now penetrated virtually every country on earth. The last bastions against global brands are gradually falling. Research by Gallup into the brand awareness of the Chinese found that Coke was already the second most popular brand, following Hitachi. While the Chinese don't, as yet, have the money or the opportunity, they do have the aspirations. They are also fully aware of the power of brands as the profusion of imitation and copying shows. (In a sign of the times, the Japanese dominated the top ten brands identified by the Chinese and only one European company, Nestlé, managed to get into the top 20.)

The importance of global brands was summed up by Unilever chairman Michael Perry:

> *'The first question to be asked of any successful brand today any-where is, will it travel? And how fast will it travel? Because you have no time to take this process slowly but surely. If you don't move that successful brand around the world rapidly you can be sure your competitor will take the idea, lift it and move it ahead of you. Speed to market is of the essence. But the point ... central to all of this is a global brand is simply a local brand reproduced many times.'*[1]

Globalisation has been fuelled by technology, international travel and the rise of truly mass media. But, it is nothing new to the world of brands. Take the story behind Hilton hotels. The realisation of the group's founder Conrad Hilton was that hotels were not just used by holiday-makers, but were temporary homes and offices for the travelling foot soldiers of the business world. In response, Hiltons offered high quality standardised service. While other hotels crumbled through the competition from motels, Hilton invented a lucrative business. Senior managers still flock to Hiltons. The global and standardised brand remains firmly in place; the Hilton in Miami is the same as that in Rome or elsewhere. Indeed the company's advertising features a taxi in a city with the caption 'Take me to the Hilton' – the assumption is that any major city will have a Hilton 'where you can be yourself again'.

Coke

Coke is the best known global brand. Currently it is available in virtually every country in the world; the only exceptions are Libya, Iran and Cuba where its absence is a matter of politics rather than taste.

It is easy to assume that Coke became a global brand effortlessly in less sophisticated times. In fact, it became a global brand for a number of reasons. First, it backed the brand from the very start. Coke's inventor, John Styth Pemberton, spent $73.96 on banners and advertising coupons during his first year selling his 'Brain and Nerve Tonic'. This budget was set against gross revenues of less than $50. Later, Coke advertisements progressed to Georgia school reports.

The next stage was the creation of the eponymous bottle. The curvaceous Coke bottle is one of the great images of the twentieth century. Of course, Coke hasn't actually used the bottle for a number of years but it is indelibly printed on our minds. Indeed, if you buy a can of Coke there is still a picture of the bottle just to remind you of its beauty. The bottle was the result of a design competition held in 1915 and won by the Root Glass Company. The Coke president, Asa Cantler, said: 'We need a bottle which a person will recognise as Coca-Cola even when he feels it in the dark.' The bottle differentiated the brand and added to the brand's identity.

Coke continued to develop people's awareness of the product. Its Coke Bathing Girls calendars were a fixture in American drugs stores during the 1930s. Internationally, its reputation was cemented during the Second World War when it boldly and ambitiously promised that any US soldier would be able to buy a Coke for a nickel. The Coke became the symbol of American taste and consumption. To fulfil its promise, Coke built 60 mobile bottling plants and sent them along with the army. Each could be run by two men and produce 1,370 bottles an hour.

There are many other successful global brands. The Mars bar is the same, no matter where you buy and eat it; the name Nescafé will get you a coffee anywhere in the world (though, interestingly, there are more than 100 varieties of Nescafé as the product and advertising are adapted to individual countries).

Benefits of globalisation

More generally, the benefits of globalisation cover five key areas of any business: R&D, Purchasing, Production, Marketing, and Distribution/sales.

Research and development

If R&D is organised on a global basis and aimed toward global markets this should allow an organisation to simplify its product range, move more quickly to meet market needs, and be more efficient through mutual co-operation.

Purchasing

Global purchasing can allow companies to respond quickly to changes in the markets for their raw materials, move more quickly to meet customer needs, and to flex their purchasing power more effectively (such as in making the most of currency dealings).

Production

If production is organised on a global basis to better meet the needs of customers it can bring economies of scale and cost reductions.

Marketing

In theory, global marketing can allow a company to make more cost-effective use of global media, save costs by eliminating duplication, and share knowledge and experience more easily. Unfortunately, such dreams are rarely matched by reality.

Distribution/sales

With systems geared to servicing a global market, a company's range of products and services should be more readily and more quickly available anywhere in the world. In addition, after-sales service should be improved – no more long waits of three months for a spare part – plus IT should enable speedy problem solving.

Globalisation, it is thought, brings speed, flexibility and cost savings. The company is in tune with and close to all of its markets no matter where they are located.

Globalisation tends, in corporate terms, to be synonymous with rationalisation. Economies of scale mean that someone somewhere is out of a job. In the first rush to brand globalisation companies have tended to take the same approach to brands. Companies with extensive brand portfolios have closely examined the cost of running and promoting large numbers of brands. If one brand costs £X to promote and ten brands costs $10X, then surely it makes sense to put all ten under a single corporate umbrella brand and concentrate the marketing expenditure there.

Owners Abroad, for example, condensed its many disparate brands under the First Choice identity and Cadbury's products are Cadbury first, product name second. This has encouraged a new focus on developing the corporate brand and, increasingly, viewing its communication from the consumer's point of view.

The benefits of global branding are all highly attractive. So attractive that there is the temptation to treat everything as a global brand. But global branding is not necessarily suitable for every product in every market. Indeed, this is far from being the case. Globalisation or global branding is not a cure for all known organisational ills. Indeed, it is often used as a placebo with managers espousing that they are truly global in outlook and practice while continuing to operate in much the same way as before.

It is also worth noting that globalisation affects all businesses even ones which remain solely in their national market.

'Their company will now face greater competition from others selling into many different markets, who have an advantage over the national manager in that they have the ability to pick up on new ideas and experience from other markets',

says Annik Hoog, co-author of *The Marketing Challenge*. 'Marketing, after all, is all about good ideas, and you shouldn't be constantly reinventing the wheel.'

While its repercussions are widespread, clearly global branding also comes with an array of potential problems. From a logistical point of view, legislative differences are, despite the Single European Market, still major factors in global brand management. Broadcasting laws are many and varied throughout Europe. What is acceptable in one country may well be anathema elsewhere. In France, for example, supermarket petrol stations cannot advertise on television thanks to a ban on advertising by the distribution sector. Despite such difficulties there is little doubt that global branding is now part of branding life and the direction in which many brands are heading.

More of the same

The first key driver to the globalisation of brands is the fact that markets are becoming more homogeneous. Thanks to increased international travel, technology and the mass media, markets are now more similar than ever before. Our spending and consumption habits in many areas are similar no matter where we live. Homogeneous markets lead inexorably to homogeneous brands.

As a result of these trends it is easier and commercially logical to create brands which cover greater areas. It is a simple argument of economy of scale. If the same advertisement will work in Italy and Finland, you don't need to make two. (Of course, working in foreign languages produces predictable troubles which should never be underestimated. Nike's 'Just do it' slogan, for example, cannot be easily translated into French, the result is the French slogan 'Ta vie est à toi' – your life is your own.)

A television commercial can cost hundreds of thousands of pounds so making one or two rather than 12 represents a huge saving. The essential things to avoid are dialogue and jokes, and it is useful to concentrate on the visual look rather than cramming a complex plot into 30 seconds. Some brands make global advertisements with small local adaptations, these include Ariel and Gillette, for example.

Similarly, if the Spanish product can have the same packaging as the French, then there is a substantial cost saving. The only thing the company needs to ensure is that the advertising or packaging works successfully in particular countries and markets. This essential detail is often one which is overlooked by companies intent on cost savings rather than brand development.

Despite the obvious and growing commercial appeal, the issue of homogeneous markets is contentious. In Europe, for example, the entire issue of sovereignty and national identity is deeply political. In a nationally splintered area like Europe most brands inevitably began life as local brands. Local brands either remain thoroughly local or develop outwards. There is no middle ground. Those which choose the latter route are pushing Europe towards a greater degree of homogenisation. This process can be contrasted with what has happened in the US where companies had a huge fairly homogeneous market on their doorstep and were quick to attempt to satisfy it. Often their attempts at developing brands in Europe quickly ran aground as they tried to enforce the same level of homogenisation on the diverse European market. Now American companies tend to be more realistic and concentrate on more localised marketing and advertising – typically, the management of Playtex in Europe is now separate from the US and there is a far greater degree of autonomy in European subsidiaries than was previously the case.

We have the technology

Many global brands are driven by technology (Sony is one good example) and Harvard's Ted Levitt has argued that technology is the most potent force in the drive towards homogenisation.

Technology is clearly a key driver to globalisation in markets such as drugs and cosmetics. In cosmetics the brand specialists arrived relatively late. BAT bought up cosmetics companies in the 1960s in an effort to transfer its brand management expertise in tobacco to the world of fragrance. The two proved mutually incompatible and British-American Cosmetics was sold off. In the 1980s, Unilever identified cosmetics as an area of potential growth and backed its enthusiasm with investment in Elizabeth Arden ($1.5 billion), Chesebrough-Ponds and Calvin Klein Cosmetics ($306 million). P&G also followed with the purchase of Max Factor. While learning that cosmetic brands behave in different ways from soap powders, Unilever has rationalised and reorganised distribution so that there is a single distribution point in Europe for Elizabeth Arden products (rather than 12). The products are made in Virginia and a small number of European sites. The global structure of the company matches the global nature of the brand.

Technology, internationalisation and homogeneity meet in what has been labelled the rise of the international lifestyle. This is one of the alluring inventions of colour magazines and marketing executives. It is based on the idea that the affluent know no international boundaries, and nor does their wealth. Luxury brands, therefore, are among the most enthusiastic practitioners of globalisation. These include cosmetics companies such as Dior or Lancôme, as well as Rolex, and the like. Their strength is such that the luxury goods sector remained steadfastly buoyant during the last recession and emerged from it stronger than many other businesses.

It has been explained by Calvin Klein himself with touching simplicity:

> 'I've lived most of my life in New York and I design for the women I know. I thought this sort of modern, working, liberated woman was mainly found on my side of the Atlantic. What I have discovered to my great surprise is that women all over the world now want to dress that way.'

Klein's discovery that lifestyle is international has certainly proved worth while, the Calvin Klein fragrance business, now owned by Unilever, turns over half a billion dollars.

It is not only the rich who have adopted what is called the international lifestyle. The young are equally susceptible to liking, wearing and listening to the same things whether they live in Prague, Manchester of Stockholm. Fashions cross borders more easily than ever before, media such as MTV help things along.

The CCA Research Institute in Paris has identified 16 distinct European consumer groups. The problem for the brand, therefore, is identifying which group will buy their product and then to target it effectively. This makes the job of promoting and marketing a brand

easier in some ways, but means that there are fewer excuses when
things go wrong.

Many of the elements of the international lifestyle come together
in the appalling shopping experience which now constitutes catch-
ing a plane. Once, terminals were empty hangers with a newspaper
shop, duty-free shop and a café. You could relax and read. Now,
there is no relaxation – you shop or die. Take Heathrow's Terminal
Four. It comes complete with Bally (it sells more shoes at Heathrow
than at any other of its retail outlets in the UK); HMV; Mappin and
Webb (the Heathrow branch sells more Rolexes than any other); as
well as the usual selection of Sock Shops and book shops. The international traveller finds that the international lifestyle is now an
inescapable fact of life.

Global and local

*'You want to be able to optimise a business globally – to spe-
cialise in the production of components, to drive economies of
scale as far as you can, to rotate managers and technologists
around the world to share expertise and solve problems. But you
also want to have deep local roots everywhere you operate –
building products in the countries where you sell them, recruiting
the best local talent from the universities, working with the local
government to increase exports. If you build such an organisation, you create a business advantage that is damn difficult to
copy',*

says Percy Barnevik, chief executive, ABB,[2] one of the world's most
successful practitioners of globalisation.

Global brands can be interpreted as uniform, unbending solutions
to the needs of particular markets. But, ultimately, uniformity is not
what makes brands succeed. They do have to be consistent, but they
also have to be flexible and responsive to local needs. People have
different expectations and requirements.

Indeed, the way people use a particular product may fundamentally differ from one country to the next. Schweppes, for example, is

used as a mixer in the UK and Ireland, but as a straight drink in France and Spain. Finding a neat approach which suits the needs of both markets is practically impossible.

As Interbrand founder John Murphy says in his book, *Brand Strategy*:

> *'The trend towards international branding of goods and services is likely to continue and indeed strengthen. This, however, by no means precludes the need for sensitive brand positioning to suit local conditions.'*

Any brand which places uniformity ahead of local responsiveness is taking a substantial risk. However, brands still need to take advantage of the potential benefits of globalisation. They need to be global and local; this balancing act has spawned the appalling phrase 'glocalisation'.

Allied to this is the need for 'mass customisation'. It was Henry Ford who championed and first implemented production on a mass scale. Ford realised that quantity was central to creating a low cost product and that low prices and consistent products attracted customers. He also developed an incredibly strong brand. If we think of Ford today we still think of mass production, reliability and highly competitive prices. Ford invented mass production and also invented a brand which has stood the test of time. The Model T was always more than a product. It was a symbol of progress and prosperity, an affordable car. Ford's only error in the development of this brand was his failure to carry the brand forward. 'I've no use for a car that has more spark plugs than a cow has teats', he is reputed to have said. While Ford stuck to what he knew worked, General Motors discovered that a single corporate brand could support a regularly changing set of sub-brands. Ford laboured over a successor to the Model T. Meanwhile, Alfred P. Sloan at General Motors was launching a new model every year and names like Chevrolet and Cadillac entered into history.

In many ways the post-war decades saw few advances on the basic principles of manufacturing practised by Ford and then General Motors. Companies sought out economies of scale through mass production. Everything else – the structure of the organisation, its technology, marketing and management – was peripheral to the central truism.

In the 1980s the corporate world discovered quality or, rather, was led there by the Japanese who had made quality the cornerstone of their industrial rebirth. They then concentrated on how to best organise their activities to produce consistently high quality levels.

In the 1990s the onus has moved again. Now, mass production needs to be combined with responsiveness to individual customers. The customer is king and demanding more and more. At Panasonic Bicycle in Japan, for example, customers can specify the size, shape and colour of their chosen bike. The computer-controlled production line then does the work.

Meeting the growing demands of consumers while benefiting from global production using the latest technology is the new challenge for companies and brands. Customisation requires local and personal contact. Brands which are based on contacts with people, such as hotels and retail brands, tend to be the most locally responsive (though, having said that, all brands should consider themselves to be people-based). Such brands are better placed to adapt to local needs; Novotel, Ibis and Holiday Inn have adapted their hotel rooms in Germany to meet local expectations as to their size and comfort levels.

Of course, not all products need to be refined to local sensibilities at all. Allied Lyons has hit on a lucrative business in supplying Hungary, Poland and Russia with complete pubs. Equally improbably, it is also setting up an ice-cream factory in Moscow. The John Bull pub is exported in a container and then erected to become an accurate, though basic, reincarnation of the great British pub.

Global with relish?

One of the best known global brands must be McDonald's. McDonald's is a brilliant international exercise in uniformity. Wherever you go in Europe or the world a McDonald's restaurant appears very similar and its products are uncanny reproductions of each other. It is homogeneous, uniform and highly successful. There is a McDonald's formula.

While McDonald's is successful across the world there is nothing particularly original or innovative about what it does. You don't have to be one of the Le Roux brothers to serve up a tasty cheeseburger. Instead McDonald's does the simple things well. Its restaurants are clean; the food is consistent; the service is good. When McDonald's began, its inspirational founder Ray Kroc decided that these elements would differentiate McDonald's from all the other burger chains. 'It requires a certain kind of mind to see beauty in a hamburger bun,' reflected Kroc. He was right, no-one else manages to do the simple things as well. In effect, the very uniformity of the brand is the crucial differentiating factor.

But also vital to the success of McDonald's is the fact that it tailors what it does to local conditions, to a limited extent and in a carefully controlled way. Staff are local – you don't find American managers laying down the law in the Madrid McDonald's. There is also some variation in the menu – it is not much, but it is varied according to local tastes. The basics remain, but McDonald's adds a salad bar or a special drink to meet local requirements. It is a global brand which appeals to global needs – reliability, cleanliness, speed and value – with a few local extras which give a sense (however small) of local identity.

Combining global and local elements is a minefield. Cultural and regional differences in Europe cannot be underestimated. For example, market research company Mintel found that 22 per cent of French people are likely to sample a product if it is endorsed by a celebrity. The British remain studiously unimpressed, only 1 per cent said they would be influenced. This, of course, begs the question as to why television advertisements in the UK consistently use a host of minor celebrities.

Different angles work in different countries. The Spanish, for example, are attracted by anything to do with sport or modernity. But it is not only national tastes and preoccupations which the brand must play to. Approaches may differ according to a brand's place and standing in the marketplace in an individual country. The soft drink Orangina, for example, is positioned and priced differently in various countries. It is a global brand which is highly responsive to local markets. In France, for example, it is highly popular (the second soft drink after Coke) while in the UK it competes as a premium brand in the orange carbonated soft drink market against local brands such as Tango or Sunkist. From an organisational point of view, strength in a particular national market generally means that the brand is given greater independence – the local rather than global is emphasised.

Going global

In the 1980s many brands leapt enthusiastically into global mode. This was particularly clear in their packaging. By way of proving their international perspective, companies suddenly insisted on printing ingredients in five languages. As you tucked into your tasty yoghurt you could contemplate the Italian word for flavourings. Fortunately such linguistic enthusiasm seems to have waned. Packaging no longer contains Greek versions of the calorific content written in microscopically small writing so that the Swedish version can also be squeezed on.

In the quest for a global brand, packaging is often the first port of call. Also high on the list is the physical identity (the logo and name) of the brand. In the process of mergers, or of geographical extension, companies have become muddled with similar products having different names. There is, as a result, a desire for simplifi-cation; for example, Shell now calls all its motor oil in Europe, Helix.

Research by Jean-Noel Kapferer of Groupe ESC in France found that only 29 per cent of companies have globalised their advertising. Activities such as sales promotion and direct marketing are always adapted to local requirements. Kapferer also found a lack of homogeneity of pricing explained by the objective of maximising profits locally.

Making brands work demands a high degree of flexibility. The more global a brand's aspirations, the more flexibility is required.

The Volkswagen Golf, for instance, does not have the same advertising (nor even name) across different countries. The brand does, however, have a strong and recognisable style which is more easily transferable than advertisements or language across different countries.

There must clearly be some sort of bonding which can stretch around the world. It may be a common style (such as for the Golf); global packaging (the linguistic nightmare); or simply a trademark or symbol used on all of a company's products.

Getting the name right

Establishing the common bond often, though not inevitably, returns brands to semantics and linguistics. Getting the name right is one of the most troublesome areas to any brand with global pretensions. Indeed, it has been suggested that the root of the problem with Persil Power (see Chapter 9) was that while Persil was feminine, Persil Power was essentially male – a change in emphasis which consumers weren't comfortable with.

After a period of dramatic instability, the Saatchi & Saatchi advertising group changed its name to Cordiant. The name was invented and, therefore, entirely meaningless. (On the plus side, this means that it is meaningless globally.) Its aim, the company explained, was to communicate 'the new spirit within the company characterised by accord and shared purpose'. The corporate identity company Siegel & Gale added that Cordiant was derived from the Latin for heart. The company went on to say that the name 'expresses a core or heart position … at the centre of one of the world's leading communications groups'.

When ICI decided to split itself into two companies it brought in a consultancy to examine the possible names for the offshoot. It took 25 people and a computer working for 14 weeks to come up with the name Zeneca. Was it worth it?

Of course, the easy answer is no. Zeneca is, to all intents and purposes, as meaningless as Cordiant. But what if they had got it wrong? What if Zeneca meant something offensive in Hebrew, thus annoying Jewish customers, suppliers and employees throughout the world? Clearly, getting the name right is highly important.

It is not, despite what consultants might say, a precise art. In the First World War the French called the Germans *boche*. It was not a term of endearment. Yet, after the war, the German company Bosch was highly successful in France. Similarly, Rentokil is not an ideal name for a company which is trying to expand into other areas rather than pest control, but it is the name we know and may well trust. (Rentokil's chief executive ignored the advice of consultants to alter the name.)

The potential for international misunderstanding is huge. Pschitt is a French drink which was actually launched in the English-speaking market and speedily withdrawn, Bum is a pack of crisps in Spain and Bimbo a loaf of bread, while Durex is sellotape in Australia.

The safest route is to do what others do. In the computer industry – supposedly full of bright and highly creative people at the leading edge of human thought – there are those with initials (IBM, ICL); companies inspired by fruit (Apple, Apricot); and those which have meaningless high-tech names (Compaq, Unisys). Occasionally names make people think twice – Apple's name, at the time, was an inspired choice. It contrasted the company with stuffy old IBM with its staid initials and corporate suits. Any differentiation enjoyed by Apple has long since evaporated, copycat names such as Apricot emerged and the name Apple is now as established as IBM.

Perhaps the best approach is the one used by the Japanese – democracy. This is certainly cheaper than employing consultants and has a good track record. The name Toyota emerged from a competition run by the company's founder Kiichiro Toyoda; Toyota in Japanese characters conveys speed and uses eight strokes, a number suggesting prosperity. From the Western perspective it is pronounceable and attractively meaningless.

Building Bud

It is estimated that the Budweiser brand is the sixth most valuable global brand ($8.2 billion) and far ahead of any other beer brand. The single beer (Budweiser) commands 5 per cent of the world beer market. Budweiser, together with other beers made by Anheuser-Busch, accounts for almost 10 per cent of the total volume of beer consumed worldwide.

Like many of the other top global brands, Budweiser has its origins in the US. Importantly, despite expansion worldwide, it has retained the brand's American roots. Perhaps its most significant achievement is to have developed into a global brand while adapting to the needs of local markets and retaining the integrity of the brand's core values.

Anheuser-Busch is by far the largest brewer in the world, with control of 44.4 per cent of the US market. It began the journey of international expansion using Budweiser as its flagship brand at the beginning of the 1980s. In 1981 Anheuser-Busch (A-B) formed an international division and began the process of selling Budweiser beer in the international marketplace. Thirteen years on, A-B products are to be found throughout the world, including 22 European countries.

From a strategic perspective, Christopher Stainow, managing director of A-B European Trade, identifies three aspects of the brand's international development:

- Budweiser positioning: making Budweiser a global *icon* brand.
- Country priorities: utilising different marketing campaigns which take into account the landscape of the local market – current size, competitive analysis, potential long-term growth, consumer trends.

This local sensitivity has remained a prime objective throughout the development of the Budweiser brand worldwide.

- Exchange of best practices: learning the local market practices and sharing experiences in order to develop strong and innovative marketing efforts.

Anheuser-Busch defines an icon in two ways: as a visual representation of an ideology or symbolic world and as a trademark that represents more than simply a brand name.

In the UK, Budweiser is seen as the pre-eminent US beer, embodying US indigenous craft and tradition, while offering consumers the possibility of partaking in a genuine, attractive and uniquely American proposition.

Related to this lifestyle offering there are a number of other elements, such as the enjoyment of American sports, like American football and drag racing, and music. When approaching the UK, A-B had to consider two fundamental issues:

1 The brand image of Budweiser: the type of person who drinks the beer. This had to be considered in the context of the local perceptions of America, its people, places and culture.

2 The product image of Budweiser: what the likely reaction of UK consumers would be to the beer in terms of its taste, appearance and quality.

Vital to this was the realisation that consumers would form an opinion of Budweiser in conjunction with their personal and ideological views of America. Potentially this could work for or against A-B.

Sometimes these perceptions are good. America is vast, free and independent and has a certain 'cool' appeal particularly to younger adults. Americans are honest, adventurous, relaxed and straightforward.

But, rightly or wrongly, perceptions of the US can be negative. America can be seen as the proponent and the origin of the 'junk' fast-food and faddish culture. Americans are sometimes seen as aggressive, arrogant and with little regard for the cultural nuances and mores of countries and cultures outside of the US.

'These countering viewpoints have an impact on how Budweiser is positioned in a particular market and how A-B's brand equity is protected in this marketplace', says Christopher Stainow.

'Anheuser-Busch is seen as a big company with strong values based around family ownership. On the other hand, American

beer is seen as weaker tasting than a standard European-style beer. The American brewing industry is also seen (in some quarters) as having few brewing credentials. In some areas as well, there is opposition to the prospect of a large American corporation establishing itself in Europe and using its considerable marketing skills and spending power to sell its products to local consumers.'

In either case, whether it is its brand or product image, the fact that A-B comes from America has an impact on the image which local beer drinkers have of its brands. In the absence of knowledge, it would have been entirely possible for drinkers to develop only a negative view of Budweiser. The same is probably true for Marlboro and McDonald's when they first embarked on international expansion.

Anheuser-Busch sought to achieve the same level of success. Bridging the gap between international strength and local awareness was based on five critical components which underpin the company's brand positioning: a positioning statement, visuals and slogans, brand personality, scale, and a strapline.

A positioning statement

These are words which define what A-B wants the brand to represent and which become the basis for all its marketing activity. The statement could be summed up as follows:

- Budweiser is a premium quality beer with a distinctively refreshing taste.
- Budweiser represents and lets beer drinkers in other countries be a part of the American image they like.
- Budweiser is a popular beer worldwide.

Visuals and slogans

A library of visual icons which represents Budweiser's symbolic world:

- The label, widely recognised and very American with its red, white and blue colours.
- The Budweiser bow tie.
- The long-neck bottle, distinctively American in its shape.
- The slogans *King of Beers* (used for over 100 years) and *The Genuine Article* which denotes the beer's sense of authenticity.

Brand personality

A series of images which provide a basis for local beer drinkers to relate to the brand.

The Budweiser brand personality could be defined as all-American, masculine, active, social and genuine – consistent with a premium quality image.

Scale

Marketing that addresses consumer expectations of a *big brand*:

- A-B's scale relies on aggressive distribution and point-of-sale merchandising; and
- association with large-scale events such as the Soccer World Cup.

A strapline

A strapline embodies the brand essence, for example:

- *The Genuine Article*
- *World's largest selling beer*
- *King of Beers*
- *This Bud's for you*
- *The best reason in the world to drink beer.*

Aside from building a strong and growing relationship with its consumers, A-B puts an enormous value on building and maintaining meaningful business relationships with its trade partners and customers.

Successful international expansion depends on more than advertising and marketing. Commitment to the local marketplace entails strong ties with the local trade in order to move the product to the consumer through wholesaler and retailer channels.

Anheuser-Busch in the UK operates in a distinctive business environment, distinctive in the priority that trade partnerships play in its success. It works closely with Courage which brews Budweiser on its behalf and with a whole network of national and regional brewers, wholesalers and retailers. In marketing the brand, Budweiser frequently seeks co-promotional platforms with a range of partners, such as the 1994 Soccer World Cup.

A-B's worldwide positioning, as well as Budweiser's brand equity, acts as a considerable incentive for the UK drinks industry to do business with it, and continues to do so regardless of shifts in the industry.

It is apparent that in the UK as elsewhere productive trade relations commands a high priority in A-B's list of business imperatives. 'Making friends is our business', says the A-B chief executive.

A-B's approach to business in the local marketplace is an expression of the brand equity and momentum delivered by the US and international marketing activity. This can manifest itself both in relations with Budweiser consumers and also trade partners of Anheuser-Busch. As David Aaker says in his book, *Managing Brand Equity*:

> '*Brand equity can provide leverage in the distribution channel. Like customers, the trade has less uncertainty dealing with a proven brand name that has already achieved recognition and associations.*'

Christopher Stainow identifies partnerships as vital commercial weapons:

> '*A strong brand will have an edge in gaining both shelf facings and co-operation in implementing marketing programmes. Without these valued trade partnerships, the goal of building Bud-*

weiser into a global icon brand would be far more difficult. Bud-
weiser is now the number two premium packaged lager in the
UK.'

The art of patience

With their huge financial strength, truly global brands might expect
national markets to open magically in front of them. As Budweiser
proves, life isn't like that. Moving into a national market, however
small, is never a foregone conclusion.

First, it requires a long-term perspective and a willingness to be
patient. Castrol, for example, set up a joint venture in Thailand in
1972. During the next 20 years development was limited. Government price controls were restrictive. Instead of withdrawing from
the market, Castrol established a distribution network and began to
build its reputation among the people it identified as a key market,
motorcyclists.

At the end of the 1980s, Castrol's patience was rewarded when
the number of Thai motorcyclists increased massively from one to
five million. Castrol now leads the market. Similarly, Castrol
remained in India long after its competitors had closed down their
offices. It now has 10 per cent of the lubrication market and its volumes have grown by 50 per cent in two years.

Harvard's Michael Porter labelled Castrol's approach 'multi-
domestic branding'. In practice this means that the strengths of the
brand are not automatically foisted on any new brand acquired by
the company. Neither is the brand management of Castrol identical
in every market – an advertisement in Chile, for example, portrayed
Castrol as the sole survivor of a nuclear holocaust. In Chile it
worked, though it would have been unlikely to in other countries.
The reason for this is unlikely to be fully understood.

Similarly patient is Allied Lyons. Its brands include Ballantine's
whisky, Kahlua liqueur, Beefeater gin and many others. It has a partnership with Japan's Suntory which allows it access to other Far
Eastern markets. (Interestingly, Suntory makes whisky which is

unavailable in the UK but this has not stopped Suntory sponsoring a prestigious golf tournament in the UK for many years at huge expense. This could be patience or indulgence.) Allied has three offices in China, a market it regards as one of huge potential. Its offices do little more than wait until the Chinese are ready.

Local difficulties

Small local difficulties can be extremely damaging. The sixteenth largest global spirits brand, for example, is an unfamiliar name: Bagpiper. Its Scottish allusion is obvious, but it is in fact the most popular Indian brand of whisky which has grown at an average rate of 20 per cent year in the 1990s. In whisky terms Bagpiper is only outranked by Johnnie Walker Red Label, J&B Rare, and Ballantine's. The disadvantage of these global brands is that they are premium products with premium prices to match. In India Bagpiper costs around $4 a bottle, while a bottle of an imported brand is likely to cost seven times as much.

Similar problems can be found in many other markets. To a large extent they are local irritations, the like of Johnnie Walker is not going to compete with Bagpiper. They only become serious issues when the local product deliberately imitates the global brand.

This is a growing problem for a huge number of branded products. Groups such as International Distillers and Vintners (IDV) and Guinness are waging a constant war against increasingly sophisticated imitations. The imitators are unburdened by such considerations as the quality of the product. Nor do they need to invest in marketing and advertising, the famous brand does that for them. Their only risk is being found out. All the major brands adopt a rigorous approach to tracing and taking legal action against counterfeiters. In recent cases in Holland 100,000 bottles of Smirnovskaya were ordered to be destroyed and the Spanish producer of an imitation of Bailey's lost a multi-million pound court case to its real makers IDV.

In the hands of the counterfeiters famous brand names become subtly, and unsubtly, altered:

- **Ouzo 12** becomes Ouzo 21: in Greece there is only one brand of ouzo worth drinking (and likely not to destroy all your mental faculties with immediate effect). The problem is that after a single glass, the numbers can easily become confusing. The clever counterfeiters are obviously keen drinkers.

- **Malibu** is transformed into Marabou: a poor copy with the bottle far from authentic in appearance. It is interesting how copiers often choose names which resemble how you would pronounce the world famous brand if you had drunk an entire bottle of it.

- **Bailey's** is shortened to Bailes: the bottle is similar, but the product is one letter short of a cream liqueur.

- **Tia Maria** appears in various guises as Zia Marina, Tia Lia and Bella Maria: while foreign sounding names appear good ideas, they offer many possibilities for the imaginative copier.

- **Johnnie Walker** is comically Johnnie Hawker, Joe Worker and Johnny Black: the traditional kind of international whiskies are more open to counterfeiting than most. It is not a practice United Distillers views lightly.

Notes

[1] Quoted in AdWeek, 14 December 1992.
[2] Taylor, W., 'The logic of global business: an interview with ABB's Percy Barnevik', *Harvard Business Review*, March–April 1991, © copyright 1991 by the President and Fellows of Harvard College. All rights reserved.

9

THE PERILS OF POWER: SOAP WARS

In 1994 Israel and Palestine reached an astonishing peace accord, and following years of struggle in Northern Ireland, peace suddenly seemed achievable. Yet, while peace was breaking out in the most unlikely of places, two of the world's largest companies were engaged in a commercial war which set new records for bitterness and threw a European industry worth £6 billion into unprecedented turmoil.

UNILEVER v PROCTER & GAMBLE

As with most wars, the seeds of the discord were apparently negligible. In fact they are barely discernible to the uneducated eye – minuscule crystals of manganese. But it was these pink crystals which led to an expensive and long-running war between the Anglo-Dutch giant Unilever and its traditional rival Procter & Gamble. The chairman of Unilever's UK business, Sir Michael Perry, later called it 'the greatest marketing setback we've seen'.

Background to the conflict

While P&G and Unilever have been involved in fiercesome competition for many decades, it has always embodied a kind of Corinthian concept of good sportsmanship. The two giants have allowed their expensive advertising to speak for itself: in 1993

Unilever spent £18.8 million advertising Persil and P&G £22.3 million on Ariel.'. They have not sought a high profile for their businesses and, perhaps surprisingly, have actually shared information and know-how.

This began to unravel in February 1994 when Unilever launched its new Omo Power and Persil Power detergents in three European countries. The marketing plan was for a rapid and highly expensive launch in 11 European countries in rapid succession.

In the world of detergents, the consumer could be excused for thinking this was not a significant event. After all, supermarket shelves were already sagging under the plethora of new products launched by manufacturers in the last few years. Unilever claimed that the new product (labelled either Omo or Persil in different European countries) was a huge technological leap forward: 'We always knew it would start a washing revolution. We just didn't expect it to start a war', a statement from the company later observed.

Unilever saw the new product as the way of striking back at P&G's growing pre-eminence in the market for fabric detergents. Unilever had been slow to exploit growing demand for concentrated products and required a major technological development to regain lost ground. Power was seen as a dramatic means of breaking through the mass of products on the market. It could, said Unilever, clean more effectively and at lower temperatures. In financial terms it represented a £200 million stake from Unilever to recapture the initiative.

The crucial crystals in Power were manganese. This was something P&G had tested and found could attack fabrics and accelerate bleaching. It had, as a result, put a stop to its research. Unilever, however, had carried gamely on, optimistic that it could eventually find a solution. It thought it had done so – in the new products manganese was used as a catalyst to increase the cleaning power of the detergent.

Claims and counter-claims

The launch of the new product did apparently give Unilever the leap forward it needed. P&G's new detergent (Ariel Future) was not scheduled to be launched until later in 1994, and the Power detergent appeared to be highly effective in removing stains. P&G quickly began examining the ingredients of the new Unilever detergent. Its research suggested that the new Power products created holes in clothes after repeated washing. If this was not controversial enough, P&G also claimed that the manganese was actually retained by the clothes so that even if washed in other detergents the effect would continue. P&G's claims sparked off a war.

At the beginning of June, Unilever pointed to increased UK market share as clear evidence that it was winning the war. It said that Persil Power's share of the UK market had risen from 7 to 10 per cent in recent weeks and its share of the concentrated detergents market had risen from 20 to 30 per cent. Even so, Unilever also confirmed that it planned to reduce the quantity of manganese in its detergent and was already making plans for a replacement product in case of disaster. P&G retaliated with claims that even at one-tenth of initial levels it would still cause abnormal wear and tear on clothes washed. At the same time, a leading Dutch supermarket chain was considering withdrawing the Power product from its shelves.

The next front was opened when, in July, Unilever said it had a copy of the draft sales brochure and a sample of P&G's new detergent, Ariel Future, which P&G planned to launch in Germany in the autumn and then the rest of Europe.

Unilever proclaimed that its examination of the brochure and sample showed that P&G's offensive against the Power products was simply a matter of corporate pique; Unilever claimed that P&G had simply been pipped at the post. 'I think this is something they've been intending to do for a long time but we got in a bit sooner than they thought we would. You realise how galling it must be to have somebody do it before you', said Andrew Seth, head of Unilever's UK detergent business.[2]

In response, P&G claimed Ariel Future 'is not a copy-cat product but a leap-frog product' and pointed out that it would not include any manganese and none had actually been produced. In a descriptive aside to the vituperative series of advertisements and press releases, a P&G spokesman is reported to have observed that with Persil Power, Unilever 'stuck a rocket motor on a Ford Cortina. The detergent can't take the power ... . With Future, we've redesigned the car from the wheel nuts up'.[3]

By August the battle was at its worst. Unilever attacked. It claimed that Power products were environmentally friendlier than competing products. Manufacturing the powder, it said, took 80 per cent less energy, achieved by only using dry ingredients, rather than having to dry them. It also argued that the product allowed consumers to wash clothes at a lower temperature – this, said Unilever, could save about 5 per cent in electricity consumption, about £3 a year. It also made direct comparisons with Ariel Ultra, the P&G competitor, claiming that 30 washes required 2.35 kilograms of Power and 2.8kg of Ariel Ultra.

Advertisements from P&G continued to ram the message home: 'Only Ariel washes so clean yet so safe' it proclaimed with warnings that the manganese accelerator could leave residues on clothes and continue to cause fading. Its advertisements led to complaints to the Advertising Standards Authority by Unilever challenging the test results and disputing P&G's claims of Ariel's superiority.

Unilever took a full-page advertisement in the *Financial Times*. Under the heading 'Why this aerial bombardment?' it said:

Sorry about the warfare. It wasn't our idea.

Our idea was simply for a better washing powder. We call it Persil Power. Families all over Britain have already used it for more than fifty million washes. And they love the results.

Meanwhile, we asked independent test institutes to compare Persil Power with another leading concentrated powder. They found no visible sign of fabric damage with either product.

Some of them did find a difference, even so. And that difference was Persil Power's significantly superior cleaning performance.

So use Persil Power with confidence. We always knew it would start a washing revolution. We just didn't expect it to start a war.[4]

At this stage Unilever appeared to be weathering the storm. Indeed, in August 1994, it announced that it had increased its share in the washing powder market in the UK and France despite the raging controversy. Profits were up to £1.06 billion in the first half of 1994. The market research company Nielsen produced more supportive statistics – it showed that the Persil brand had increased its overall UK market share from 27 per cent to 28.2 per cent since the launch of Persil Power. At the same time, P&G's Ariel had slipped from 29 to 26.4 per cent of the market. In the concentrated market, Ariel was still in the lead, though Persil had increased its share from 6 to 9 per cent.

Unilever admitted that sales had been disappointing in Scandinavia, Switzerland and the Netherlands, though had been stronger in France and the UK.

In September the claims and counter-claims continued with an outbreak of reports. A report from the Dutch consumers' association was critical of Power, claiming that some fabrics were 'damaged' in the test. 'The data is partial and being used in a very emotive way', countered Unilever. P&G European vice-president of communications, David Veitch, not surprisingly took another view: 'This cannot come as any surprise in light of the evidence that has already emerged.'[5]

In November, P&G launched its new product Ariel Futur (or Future in the UK). It marked, claimed P&G, 'a considerable technological advance in washing powders'.[6] Backed by a £7 million television advertising campaign in the UK, Future hit the shops in January 1995. In the same month Unilever announced that it was planning to launch a new flagship detergent, New Generation Persil. The new product, it said, was more effective at cleaning and less damaging than Ariel Future, and, most importantly, did not include any pink crystals.

LESSONS FROM THE WASH

Announcing a rise in profits to £2.38 billion in February 1995, Unilever announced it was writing off £57 million of stock thanks to the soap war. 'The lessons have been learned and internal processes reviewed', pronounced Sir Michael Perry while Dutch chairman, Morris Takaksblat, promised 'This has put a small dent, really minimal, in our position, which we think we can fully repair.'

Given such confidence, there is a temptation to regard the soap wars as a unique incident from which few generic lessons can be learned. The two companies are corporate giants and the scale of their financial investment in brands, and the ferocity of their campaigns, is matched by few other organisations. However, there are a number of important lessons which came out in the dirty wash of the soap wars and these are discussed below.

Squaring the circle is (usually) impossible

Unilever's Power sought to defy the increasing segmentation of the market by offering a stronger and better product which could be used for a wide variety of clothes at low temperatures. It was all things to all people and, as P&G relentlessly pointed out, too good to be true. It is now downgraded to a specialist detergent for whites and use on heavily soiled clothes. In December 1994 it took less than 1 per cent of the UK detergent market.

In effect Power attempted to square the circle. It set out to revolutionise the marketplace, but was ill-equipped to do so. The message for other brands must be that to attempt a quantum leap forward demands total confidence in the product.

The product has to be good

'Technology can be a marketing curse as well as a blessing', observed the *Financial Times*.

   'Companies seize on technical innovations as a unique selling

point for products, especially in mature, oligopolistic markets, such as European detergents. Yet unless they subject their new products to the most rigorous testing ... the invention may blow up in their faces.'

Clearly, the bottom line for any brand is the product. It has to do what you will say it will do. It has to fulfil your promises and be beyond reproach. In the case of Persil Power this was clearly not the case. In many ways Unilever would have been well advised to admit the product wasn't perfect and then withdraw it. This, of course, would also have been incredibly expensive. Instead it was neither

> **The bottom line for any brand is the product. It has to do what you will say it will do. It has to fulfil your promises and be beyond reproach.**

prepared to give Power a ringing endorsement or to withdraw it. Choosing the middle ground, Unilever tinkered with the formula and this rather confirmed P&G's claims. If Unilever had simply held its collective hands up and admitted culpability, this may in the long term have enhanced its standing. Now, any of its new products are going to be routinely analysed for any defects.

Fighting dirty benefits neither side

Clearly Unilever did not emerge intact from the soap wars. But in many ways P&G's aggressive response was excessive. It went for the jugular when its victim was already bleeding to death. The Advertising Standards Authority later criticised P&G for implying that its products were superior to all others on the market – though it found that P&G's claim that its products were safer was fair.

Beware segmentation

There are now eight varieties of Persil on the market, with Persil Finesse for wool and silks. The profusion of brand extensions in the detergents market has filled supermarket shelves. The question must be whether it has benefited consumers and whether, in the long term, it will benefit the two companies.

Beware the media

What is striking about the soap wars is the column inches it generated. At times the coverage was farcical. In February 1995, long after the original formula had been withdrawn from supermarket shelves and the new formula Persil Power was fast disappearing, the UK consumers' association published the results of its research. It was critical of Persil Power, but its press conference featured people walking around with torn shirts which had been washed in the detergent no longer available. The tests cost over £50,000 and produced a suitably irrelevant postscript to a lot of froth, a deficient product and a great deal of corporate mischief making.

Notes

[1] Ariel is back as top of the soaps', *Financial Times*, 16 June 1994.
[2] Quoted in 'Unilever and Procter open new front in soap war', *Financial Times*, 18 July 1994.
[3] Quoted in 'P&G, Unilever soap wars leave market spinning', *Financial Times*, 1 November 1994.
[4] Advertisement, *Financial Times*, 6–7 August 1994.
[5] Oram, R., 'Dutch study hits at Unilever detergent', *Financial Times*, 15 September 1994.
[6] Quoted in 'P&G, Unilever soap wars leave market spinning', *Financial Times*, 1 November 1994.

10

ELASTIC BRANDS

INTRODUCTION

So, if you have invented and established a highly successful brand what do you do next? The answer, increasingly, is to apply the brand within the same business (brand extension) or to stretch the same brand to another business (brand stretching).

A typical example of the latter is Virgin which has taken on a seemingly random life of its own. Originally, Virgin was a record company. Then, a record retailer which seemed a sensible piece of brand stretching. And then it became an airline, a radio station, a cola manufacturer and, perhaps most surprisingly, a provider of financial services: one brand now combines a plethora of unrelated activities. Though it has been extended and stretched, the strength of the brand remains – we just no longer know what product area it is referring to.

BRAND EXTENSION

Brand extension is less dramatic than brand stretching and has been one of the most remarkable trends of recent years. Even the most successful brands have extended themselves:

- Coca-Cola has produced Diet Coke.
- Pepsi has Pepsi Max and Diet Pepsi.
- Marlboro aims to attract the health-conscious smoker with Marlboro Lights.

- Silk Cut, already mild, also now offers Silk Cut Mild and Silk Cut Extra Mild.

- Fosters lager comes in a number of alternatives: Fosters Draught, Fosters Export, Fosters Ice and plain ordinary Fosters.

These brand extensions are understandable; the companies are basically competing against themselves, believing that consumers will be attracted to the new product on the strength of the original brand. As well as attracting new customers, it also gives existing customers increased choice with the reassurance of the brand. If they don't like it they will return to the original.

In the tyre market, Italy's Pirelli is long established with around 14 per cent of the European tyre market: behind Michelin and Continental, but equal with Goodyear. In an effort to extend its brand, Pirelli moved into the lower end of the replacement tyre market. This was a market the company was already in chiefly through national brands, such as Courier in the UK and Create in Italy. Its new development was to begin a pan-European strategy for secondary brands.

Pirelli was not first off the grid. Virtually all of its competitors have similar approaches. The industry's basic pattern is for each company to have a premium brand. This is then supported by cheaper products which have their own brand names: Michelin has Kleber; Continental has Uniroyal Semperit; Goodyear has Kelly Springfield. These second or third tier brands compete against each other and with own-label brands.

BRAND STRETCHING

The hard bit comes when you take the leap into a completely different area: brand stretching. The leap can appear a challenging one. Zip maker, the YKK Corporation, is currently running a newspaper advertisement which boasts: 'More than just a good zipper ... our advanced architectural products are changing the face of the world'. Detecting the link is impossible.

It can be done. Yamaha, for example, uses its corporate brand on products as diverse as motorbikes, skis, organs, grand pianos, and even holiday homes. The core qualities of the organisation can apparently be placed on any product.

Take Boddingtons. Here are some suggestions for stretching the Boddingtons brand:

- Boddingtons Leisure: a range of exclusive leisure wear, only available in the colours brown and cream to reflect the original product.

- The Boddingtons Experience: a multi-million pound leisure park built around a full-scale reproduction of a Victorian brewery.

- Boddingtons Holidays: fly away safely in the hands of your favourite brewer.

The thing is it works ... up to a point. With certain products and services, attaching the name Boddingtons adds value. These are in associated business areas – making pint glasses, beer mats etc. However, once you get to Boddingtons Holidays you are beginning to wonder how the name can add value.

Brand stretching takes advantage of the fact that brands are no longer married to their products. A broader definition of brands allows a broader definition of how they can be applied, so Sony can move into markets as diverse as video tapes and mobile phones with ease (only struggling when it entered the unreal world of Hollywood). This means that there is a trend towards what have been (accurately) called 'mega-brands', giant monoliths which can attach their names and brands to virtually anything.

The basic reason for brand stretching is the increased probability of success using an established brand. Of new product launches examined by OC&C Strategy Consultants from 1984 to 1993, only 30 per cent of new brands survived at least four years, but brand extensions had more than double the survival rate, at 65 per cent. Brands which stretch themselves start from a position of some credibility and knowledge. Consumer awareness does not have to be developed from zero. This saves money and makes it more likely that the new product will succeed.

Recent examples of brand stretching include:

- Campbells has gone one step beyond meatballs to produce round hot-dog sausages, taking the shape of the meatball and applying it to a hugely successful market.

- Bisto, purveyors of gravy for Sunday lunches, has made the logical step into the rest of the week's cooking with casserole sauces.

- Flora has developed its business from margarines and spreads into salad dressings.

- Mars has made the great leap from the world of chocolate bars to ice-cream and milk drinks.

- The Japanese electronic games company Sega has built a theme part in Yokohama which boasts the name Joypolis. The park includes space-flight simulators and the Mad Bazooka ride. Sega plans to build another park in Piccadilly Circus.

Such stretching exercises make obvious commercial sense, though the element of risk remains high. Just because Mars or anyone else is hugely successful in a particular market means little elsewhere. 'A name is a rubber band, the more you stretch it, the weaker it becomes', say Al Ries and Jack Trout in *Positioning – The Battle for Your Mind*. The trouble is that companies only know when they have stretched a brand too far when the rubber band breaks.

John Bryan, chief executive of Sarah Lee, the American consumer group, has commented: 'In a free market system, people will choose to test the limits of their brands. But in the 1980s some people thought they were limitless.'

In the case of Virgin, the company's strategy does appear on the surface at least to be inconsistent. The businesses seem a million miles from each other. However, its strategy is to look at virtually any consumer market where it thinks it can undercut a sluggish and complacent brand leader with a similar product. Though its product may be similar, it believes that the strength of the Virgin brand will help boost sales to take it to a credible position in the market very quickly. The strength of the Virgin brand is such that it is highly flexible, though not that flexible that it could be associated with another of Richard Branson's ventures, Mates condoms.

Announcing a move into consumer goods, Virgin said:

'This is a big departure for us. Apart from the Body Shop, Virgin is the only new international brand to come out of Britain in the last couple of decades that has recognition in three continents. But we don't use it in any form of hard products that people can pick up.'

Interestingly, it is becoming clear that Virgin is not associated with a particular product, but with certain characteristics: good people-friendly service, the human side of business, entrepreneurial flair, combined with sound business acumen. Virgin and Richard Branson clearly enjoy being mischievous. In October 1994, for example, Branson announced with apparent sincerity that he planned to launch a drink called Virgin Mary, a tomato and tabasco mixer to go with Virgin Vodka. That he chose to make this announcement in Dublin guaranteed controversy and, inevitably, headlines.

Stretching too far

Unfortunately, for all the neatly-packaged business strategies, the last decade has often seen brands extended in a cavalier way. The profusion of brands can be seen in shampoos, biscuits and many other products. Variety abounds to a ludicrous extent. Marketers have followed the path of proliferation of brands with line extensions to the point of lunacy. There is a malt whisky branded by the Conservative Party (the label depicts former Prime Ministers); Marlboro markets a range of leisure wear which, its advertising proudly pronounces, 'fits the man'; and a host of others have moved away from their traditional area of expertise to impose their brand elsewhere.

In supermarkets the choice is overpowering. In fact, from 1985 to 1992, the number of consumer packaged goods grew at a rate of 16 per cent a year; while shelf space only grew by 1.5 per cent per year.[2]

It is little wonder that shelves appear more crowded than ever before.

So, while marketers are extending product lines and further segmenting their markets, most categories are not expanding. People are not washing their clothes more often and buying more laundry detergent because P&G and Unilever have introduced a variety of new brands. Indeed, research by Will Hamilton of Kingston Business School into the UK's top 500 consumer goods brands found more than half had experienced a decline in sales volumes between 1991 and 1994 and only 184 saw sales growth.

THE DOWN SIDE OF ELASTICITY

Brand stretching and extension can be a good idea which provides commercial benefits. But the risks are often substantial and are discussed below.

Diluting brand logic

Holiday Inn is one of the most famous hotel brand names in the world. But what do you think of when you think of Holiday Inn? The chances are that you think of quality, value and middle-of-the-road hotels. You don't consider Holiday Inns as being on a par with Hiltons for example.

In an effort to bridge this gap, Holiday Inn created a new brand through its luxury Holiday Inn Crowne Plaza hotels. The Crowne Plaza brand was intended to offer added value and all the indulgences normal Holiday Inns don't include. But in 1994 Holiday Inn did an about-turn and decided to remove the company name from the hotels so they could be marketed as a separate brand. Market research showed that Holiday Inn should not be extended to top of the range hotels. In response Holiday Inn created two new US hotel brands: Holiday Inn Select, business hotels, and Holiday Inn Hotel and Suites for longer-stay guests.[3]

The difficulty with the Holiday Inn move into luxury hotels was that its brand was simply not associated with luxury, but with value for money family hotels. Attaching the Holiday Inn name actually worked against the Crowne Plazas being perceived as top class hotels. It is the equivalent of Lada suddenly trying to market a top of the range sports car.

The brand can only be carried so far and the danger of any brand extension is that the core brand is left behind. If you think of the name Cadbury, for example, you automatically think of chocolate. But the Cadbury brand was once liberally extended and could be found on mashed potatoes, savoury snacks and canned meat. Now, Cadbury's emphasis is on nurturing the core brand rather than over-extending it. The brand's association with Britain's industrial heritage has led Cadbury to shift attention to products such as greetings cards and limited edition prints, while also franchising the name for food and drinks products. It has more closely identified what the brand stands for and is tailoring the products to fit this perception.

Confusing the consumer

For all the exciting new brands introduced by detergent makers in recent years, for many customers the result is abject confusion. As you stand in the supermarket aisle contemplating the shelves of detergents you become overwhelmed by choice and indecision. The product you have been buying for years is likely to have been repackaged in an unrecognisable way or have been pushed to one side by a new powder which is ideal for washing silk garments which have fruit juice stains.

Brand extensions can confuse customers so much that they buy a competing product.

Related to this is the fact that extending brands actually encourages consumers to be promiscuous in their purchasing behaviour. When the makers of Fosters launched Fosters Ice their message to consumers was 'You already enjoy Foster now try our new brand'. This is okay, but what it is also doing is saying 'Trying new products is a good idea ... so long as it is one of ours'. In fact, brand extension risks encouraging consumers to try different products and brands. Consumers have an array of options and are increasingly likely to shift indecisively from one to another, experimenting perpetually.

From a simple logistical angle there is a finite amount of space available on the world's supermarket shelves. Even if your new product manages to displace a rival brand it is quite likely that the end result will be less space for the core brand.

Costing more

One of the main attractions of brand extensions is cost. New brands are expensive and risky. Indeed, it is estimated that the cost of successfully launching a brand in the US is around $30 million while a line extension can cost only $5 million.

An obvious corollary of taking consumer attention away from the main brand is the fact that stretching or extending a brand is expensive. Line extensions lead to increased costs which usually results in less money being spent on the core brand. While there are still appropriate times for brand extensions, the threat of confusing the consumer, encouraging them to switch to other brands, and of empty shelves should be enough to give any marketing person pause for considerable thought.

Easily copied

Extending a product range is a move which is easily matched by competitors. The product is unlikely to be too dissimilar from the main brand.

BUILDING BUSINESS THROUGH ELASTICITY

Finding the limits of elasticity is the hard part. In the US, Coke and Pepsi have been responding to changing consumer demands by extending their brands. As people have become more health-conscious, Coke and Pepsi have introduced low-calorie and sugar-free variations on their core products. All carry the original brand name.

More recently the two cola giants have had to face emerging competition from 'New Age' soft drinks (no relation to the travellers of the same name). The leader in this field has been Snapple Beverage which sells exotically titled brands such as Mango Madness Cocktail and Raspberry Iced Tea. Snapple's success was such that it was snaffled up by Quaker Oats for a massive $1.7 billion in cash; Quaker said it wanted to concentrate some of its energies in what it called 'good-for-you' beverages.

It was at this point that both Coke and Pepsi decided that their brands, despite their legendary strength, would break. Coke set up a joint venture with Nestlé to produce iced teas under the Nestea brand, while Pepsi entered into a join venture with Thomas J. Lipton to produce iced tea.

In more direct competition to Snapple Beverage, Coke is also using the Fruitopia brand to produce the likes of Raspberry Psychic Lemonade and Grape Beyond which bear uncanny similarities to the zany names of the Snapple products.

It is still important to recognise the limits beyond which a brand and its mark cannot be moved. To reach the top end of the car market, Toyota felt the need to create a stand-alone brand, Lexus, and Ford bought Jaguar because the Ford mark, though strong, could not be credibly attached to a high performance luxury car. Similarly, Kodak has experienced some difficulty in successfully marketing its business to business product.

Cultivating the core

Coke and Pepsi's wariness about over-extending their brands is part of an increasing awareness that concentrating on core brands is a safer strategy than moving into businesses you know very little about. In the sensible 1990s the core is everything. Typically, SmithKline Beecham has defined its core as a healthcare supplier (this meant it disposed of 'non-core' businesses such as Brylcreem, Badedas bath oil and the Silvikrin and Vosene shampoos).

Cultivating the core is fashionable. But in commonsense terminology it simply means sticking to businesses you understand or in which the brand offers added value to consumers. Cultivating the core means not allowing the brand to stretch too far, something no business wants to do in the first place.

Alternatively, there are some safer options, or at least ones which mitigate the risks somewhat and these are detailed below.

Franchising

Franchising began nearly 50 years ago in the United States. It is now a huge business. In total there are estimated to be 25,000 franchise outlets in the UK run by around 400 different franchise companies. Their annual turnover is estimated at around £5 billion.

Franchising can cover a huge range of activities. In the 1990s, 8,000 franchised milk delivery rounds have been set up in the UK. There are many other opportunities: restaurant chains, printing (Prontaprint), cleaning services (such as Service Master), sandwich shops (Prêt à Manger in London now sells franchises). McDonald's, Kentucky Fried Chicken, Tie Rack, Burger King and Holiday Inn are some of the household names run as franchises. Holiday Inn has mushroomed over the last 20 years to 1,500 hotels.

Turning a brand into a franchise has a number of key attractions. It can allow the brand to become national in its coverage quickly and at minimal cost. However, some franchises have floundered when the franchise company and the franchisee have fallen out or simply failed to agree on how the business should be run. The health food chain, Holland & Barrett began selling franchises in the 1980s, but put a halt to the process after experiencing problems in managing the franchises. The trouble comes when the thorny question of who actually runs the business is not clear. While the franchise company believes it has a winning formula, the franchisee will want to do things his or her way. If a balance isn't struck the business is unlikely to satisfy either side.

Benetton is an interesting example. Its shops are franchises. The company advises on shop decor, location, advertising, and product purchases but it does not receive royalties on sales or give exclusive rights for a particular area.

Explaining the arrangement, Luciano Benetton has said:

'A Benetton shop owner agrees to sell Benetton products, we agree to take care of the image and promotion of the Benetton trademarks and guarantee speed and timeliness in the supply of our merchandise.'

The entire issue of monitoring can create problems. Franchises require a formula to be effectively shared. If the franchisor does not monitor the performance of the franchisee, there is the danger that the franchisor will make mistakes which have already been made elsewhere or head up a succession of blind alleys.

To succeed, the brand has to be strong in the first place. The stronger the brand, the more likely it is to succeed. If the franchise is built on a weak or not commonly known brand, the chances of success are reduced.

Licensing

Increasingly companies are using licensing as a means of extending their brands while mitigating the risks. The Club (once known as Club 18–30) has a range of clothes along with the fashion company Joe Bloggs. Pepsi-Cola also has a similar deal with Smith & Brooks. Camel has a fashion collection; its advertising aims to appeal to rugged, excitement seeking Indiana Jones-types.

Licensing is already a huge business, particularly in the US where licensed merchandise sales totalled $66.1 billion in 1993. It is basically a form of subliminal advertising. Advertisements for Camel's clothing collection do not feature cigarettes just the logo and the association of the brand name with adventuresome men.

Notes

[1] Quoted in 'After the feast', *The Economist*, 4 December 1993.
[2] *Harvard Business Review*, September–October 1994.
[3] 'Holiday Inn Hotels brand change', *Financial Times*, 15 September 1994.

11

COLA CONFLICT

COTT CORPORATION v COCA-COLA AND PEPSICO

Until 1994 the Toronto-based Cott Corporation was not a well-known name in the retail world. It propelled itself to the front pages, through challenging two of the world's biggest brands, Coca-Cola and PepsiCo. The result was what quickly became labelled 'the cola war'. By the end of 1994, the two goliaths weren't out for the count, but they were groggy on the ropes waiting for the bell to ring. Cott, the chirpy but unfancied challenger, has danced circles round Pepsi and Coke though whether it will continue to do so is open to serious questioning.

Background to the conflict

Cott may have called the shots in the cola war, but its roots lie in the increasing power of large retailers. The battlefields are the world's cola shelves in the supermarkets, but the war goes far beyond. The story is simple. Cott makes cola concentrate which it sells to supermarket chains and other retailers. They then market the cola under their own brand name. It may not be the real thing, but it is cheaper. Retailers can undercut the premium brands (Coke and Pepsi) while still extracting a bigger profit margin. The Cott concentrate costs as little as a sixth of that for Coke or Pepsi and the logistics allow retailers to make an extra 15 per cent profit.

The argument was simply put by Cott's chairman and chief executive Gerald Spencer: 'The bottom line is that our product sells to retailers at around $3.25 a case and theirs sells for $5 a case or more. If the products are of equal quality, why should retailers pay more?'[1]

An additional benefit for Cott is that its agreements with 90 retail chains worldwide don't involve it in any expensive advertising. Contrast this with the vast amounts spent by Pepsi and Coca-Cola in promoting their products. Coke sponsors the National Football League in the US while Pepsi picks up the bills for celebrity advertising – basketball star, Shaqille O'Neal, and more.

With minimal marketing costs and a world apparently full of willing purchasers, it is little wonder that Cott's sales and profits are soaring. Its sales have mushroomed from C$43 million in 1989 to C$665 million in 1993 and, in June 1994, its sales were up 66 per cent and profits by 67 per cent on the previous quarter.

Cott's insurrection is truly international. It sells to the largest US retailer Wal-Mart, Sainsbury's and Safeway in the UK and Ito Yokado, one of Japan's biggest retailers. The retailers simply add the brand name of their choice. Wal-Mart sells Sam's American Choice; Sainsbury's has Classic Cola; and in Canada there is Royal Crown Cola (RC Cola to its admirers).

Developments in the UK

In the UK the cola conflict has been particularly fierce and, at times, farcical. In April 1994, Sainsbury's introduced its Classic Cola. While there wasn't exactly dancing in the street when the product reached the shelves, attention began to be paid when Sainsbury's revealed how successful the new brand was. The UK cola business is estimated to be worth around £670 million every year so the stakes are high. In its first four weeks of sales, Classic Cola accounted for 60 per cent of the company's cola sales – this equals a quarter of England's entire take-home cola market. At nearly half the price of Coke and Pepsi, Classic Cola was cleaning up the market.

Not surprisingly other retailers were quickly on the phone to Cott headquarters (or, if you believe their side of the story, Cott was on the phone to them). In a move that surprised virtually every one, the next entrant into the market was Virgin Cola. The airline-radio conglomerate, signed a six-month deal with supermarket chain Tesco to distribute the cola exclusively in the UK. 'The range of drinks that

Coke sells we will be selling', promised Richard Branson.¹ It first reached Tesco's shelves on 21 November 1994. With typical ambition, Virgin said it hoped for a 10 to 15 per cent share of the total UK cola market within a year and planned to launch Virgin Cola outside the UK.

The next chain to take the plunge was Safeway, the UK's third biggest food retailer, with Safeway Select. Select was also immediately successful, helping Safeway increase own-label cola sales nine fold and total cola sales by 20 per cent.

Despite their different names, Classic Cola, Virgin Cola and Select all come from Cott, though each professes to be unique.

Response from Coca-Cola and PepsiCo

The threat from Cott has already had a dramatic effect on the financial fortunes of the cola giants. In June 1994, Pepsi's share price fell by 16 per cent in New York in ten days. Coke's Canadian bottling subsidiary closed eight of its plants and 62 of its administration offices. In some areas, Coke and Pepsi have lowered prices and increased the margins for retailers.

In the UK Coke began a £4 million advertising campaign at the end of 1994 targeted at winning customers back. With the slogan 'All colas are not the same' the campaign depicts a family in a ghostly supermarket manned by robots selling own-label products. The campaign was in response to the news that Coke's share of the UK cola market had slipped to less than 50 per cent for the first time. Indeed, figures from the market research group Taylor Nelson AGB recorded a dramatic fall from 54.6 per cent of the market in October 1994 to 42.3 per cent by the end of November.

Among the responses from Pepsi was a star-studded promotion which took 1,400 competition winners to Ibiza for a week. There they were entertained by a collection of super models and sports stars, including Magic Johnson and Pat Cash.

LESSONS FROM THE FIZZ

The cola war has many interesting and important lessons for brands in the future. The most obvious one is that financial might and traditional strength in the markets count for very little. Coke was launched in the UK in 1921 and has dominated the market ever since. Coke and Pepsi combined sell more than 50 per cent of all carbonated drinks consumed in the world – that is a lot of fizzy flavoured water. Yet, despite its huge advertising budget and its traditional leadership, customers appear to have little brand loyalty. Even if this is just a storm in a cola container, Coke has lost a large amount of money. If it is a long-term change in the market, it is looking at vastly diminished returns. Its only consolation in Europe and the UK is that per capita consumption of soft drinks is relatively low (four gallons per person per year; against 49 in the US).

The second vital lesson is that the balance of power is clearly shifting to a small number of large retailers. Companies like Sainsbury's, Safeway and Tesco have considerable, and increasing, power. In the past they were loathe to exercise it, as they concentrated on their geographical and physical development. The development of the brand was all important.

Now their brands are strong and established, the emphasis is on extracting increased profits from the shop space they have and on using their own brand within the shop as effectively as possible.

Every single item they sell must justify its existence, it must fight for shelf space. If they believe that their own-label product will make more money for them, they will stock it at the expense of the established brand. Own-label goods account for 41 per cent of sales (up 2 per cent in the last six months of 1994) at Safeway (helped by the launch of Safeway Savers, a cut-price range to counter competition from discounters).

Interestingly, the very success of own-label products may lead to the retailers marketing their own brands in a similar way to the likes of Coke and Pepsi. By 1995 Sainsbury's Classic Cola was accounting for 65 per cent of the cola the supermarket chains sold and 11 per cent of the UK market. On course to becoming one of the UK's top

50 best-selling brands, Classic Cola has already started to ape the big names by announcing a sponsorship deal with the English Basketball Association. The deal, worth £115,000, is paltry compared to the marketing expenditure of Coke and Pepsi but, even so, might be a pointer to future developments. If own-label brands become locked in a cycle of out-marketing each other, then their price competitiveness will soon disappear.

The third vital lesson is addressed by Cott chairman and chief executive Gerald Spencer: 'Consumers are smarter now than they were 20 years ago', he has observed, adding the punchline: 'You can only pay so long for an icon.'[2] Customers are more sophisticated and more demanding than ever before. More of the same is no longer enough. Their expectations are continually increasing. Companies and their brands must move to meet them, otherwise they face certain disaster.

In the case of Coke and Pepsi familiarity may, in the end, be breeding discontent. They are so successful and so omnipresent that there is the risk of appearing dull and unexciting. Indeed, recent years have seen the steady rise of competition to cola. While in the late 1980s cola accounted for 63 per cent of the US soft drinks market, by 1993 this figure was around 58 per cent as consumers experimented with new products. Even so, cola still accounts for 57 per cent of the world carbonated soft drink market (trailed dismally by lemon-lime at 13 per cent, orange at 11 per cent, with 'others' at 19 per cent).

The cola wars have probably shaken Coke and Pepsi up. Indeed, the end result will probably benefit the two giants and consumers – prices are likely to remain lower and Coke and Pepsi are likely to have become more competitive. Coke's chief marketing officer Sergio Zyman has promised more frequent new products and has summarised the company's aim as 'aggressively addressing growth opportunities wherever they exist.'[3] The company's mission is 'To put a Coke within arms reach of everyone in the world'.

Notes

1   *Financial Times*, 28–29 October 1994.
2   'Cola warriors identify new enemy', *Financial Times*, 11–12 June 1994.
3   'Tonic for Fickle Tastebuds', *Financial Times*, 24 August 1994.

12

BRANDS IN
THE ORGANISATION

INTRODUCTION

With a characteristically sage-like comment, management thinker Peter Drucker observed: 'There are no recipes for success, only failure.' Yet, recipes for success have dominated management thinking, writing and practice throughout the twentieth century. Good management is and has been available on prescription from business schools and management gurus. Generic business strategies propounded by well-paid luminaries have attracted many managers. They are told that if they do certain things they will become successful, or at least reduce the risk of failure. Complex issues, such as achieving competitiveness, are boiled down to four or five golden rules.

The way companies manage brands has proved no exception to this general trend. However, if organisations are to utilise the real power of brands this demands that managers learn new skills, more flexible ways of working and that organisations shake off their traditional ways of operating. Recipes are no more – but the menu is growing larger by the day.

The business environment is now beset with constant change. Success is increasingly elusive, however large the marketing budget. The new emphasis must, therefore, be on achieving fundamental rather than isolated changes. This runs counter to the traditional preoccupation with enhancing existing ways of working rather than developing new and radical alternatives.

The conventional outlook has placed a great deal of emphasis on learning from neat packages of history. This tendency has spawned management education by case study which tends, with hindsight, to make brand management seem a logical and clear-cut art. In today's turbulent environment, management is often anything but logical and clear – indeed, the world of brands has never been surgically precise.

How things were done yesterday is almost irrelevant. Yes, we can and must learn from past experiences and mistakes. (Though this is something managers and organisations are notoriously inept at doing.) But the lessons of the past are only practically useful if they can be applied to the new business environment. It is no good learning history if we now must study and master the international dynamics of tomorrow's technology.

MANAGING BRANDS IN THE FUTURE

In the 1990s and beyond more of the same is simply not good enough. Nor is improving and accelerating the processes and activities which have worked in the past.

> *'There's a very obvious set of conditions that plague most companies. They can see that doing what they know how to do faster and harder isn't enough to take them into the next century',*

warns management guru, Richard Pascale.[1]

The following list summarises the way forward for brand management within organisations:

- Yesterday's success is tomorrow's failure unless the brand is effectively and innovatively managed.
- How you managed and organised brands in the past will not be how you will do things in the future.
- Brands must live in and build from the present. They must be organised to make the most of today's environment to meet today's goals.

Starting with the consumer

If the organisation of the future has to be different from that of the past the difference must start with the consumer. How a company organises itself, manages its brands and manages its people begins and ends with the needs, demands and aspirations of consumers. Out of touch means out of business.

In their book *The Virtual Corporation*,[2] William Davidow and Michael Malone describe the achievements of a large number of organisations which have become extraordinarily close to customers. So close, in fact, that they regularly exceed customer expectations. 'The ideal virtual product or service is one that is produced instantaneously and customised in response to customer demand',

> **How a company organises itself, manages its brands and manages its people begins and ends with the needs, demands and aspirations of consumers.**

they write. The final product or service received by the customer is a summation of all the knowledge, processes and behaviours existing in the organisation. They are all working towards reaching a simultaneous goal when the customer walks through the door.

On a practical level, organisations need to bring more employees into direct contact with customers. People must be the living representation of brand values. Reuters, for example, increased the number of account handlers so that closer and more personal relationships could be developed with its customers. Other organisations are making similar strides to bring themselves closer to customers. This can be achieved in a myriad of ways.

UK building society Legal & General has introduced customer advisory groups made up of brokers and agents who meet at least every three months. Ideas emerging from these panels were brought together in a report 'Commitment to Customer Service' which now forms the heart of the company's quality programme. One section of the report lists 38 processes, including policy quotation, underwriting and claims settlement, and gives the company's performance over the latest and previous quarters.

In *Re-engineering the Corporation*, Michael Hammer and James Champy cite the example of the US food chain Taco Bell (a PepsiCo brand) which was losing customers fast until it decided to actually ask customers what they wanted. Customers wanted good food, served fast, in a clean environment, at a price they could afford. It seems obvious enough, but Taco Bell had got out of the habit of asking and had forgotten that customers aren't interested in the finer points of how all this is achieved.

Taco Bell decided to reduce everything except the cost of goods sold. Layers of management were eliminated, nearly every job was redefined and restaurant managers were given greater responsibility for the way their own restaurant was run. One hundred managers were put on call to solve problems in the company's 2,300 restaurants – previously there had also been 350 area managers controlling 1,800 restaurants. Taco Bell moved from a situation where 70 per cent of the restaurant was kitchen area and 30 per cent was for customers, to the exact reverse, doubling seating in the same building, with takings up substantially.

Such initiatives benefit everyone involved. They really do add value. Customers receive better service and have a more positive view of the brand. Crucially, from a corporate perspective, imaginative solutions, such as Taco Bell's, mean that market share grows without the need to make drastic cuts in prices. Instead of a price war, the company is committed to a performance war which, win or lose, benefits the bottom line.

Moving closer to customers sounds obvious, but statements of why a company is in business invariably narrow perspectives – they usually centre on a particular function or aspect of a company's business and are virtually never focused on the needs and aspirations of customers. Indeed, some appear to be built around a basic disrespect for customers.

The end result is that the **potential** demand of customers is not met. Customers are used, abused and taken for granted, rather than developed and satisfied. But what if companies took another view and started by asking what is it that customers really want?

Many already do this through rigorous market research, customer surveys and other procedures. The trouble is that though the data is there, organisations usually fail to transform their knowledge of customers into changes in the way they organise themselves or how they produce their products or services. The customer may be king but the corporation usually remains republican.

Farewell Henry Ford

Amid the maelstrom of corporate and personal change it is easy to ignore basic questions and carry on as before. This is something at which organisations are highly adept. Research has shown that companies can carry on blindly following a strategy based on a fundamental misconception for a number of years. Products and brands which people blatantly don't want have money thrown at them until, eventually, they grind to a halt (publishing is an area where this is rife; remember the *London Daily News* and James Goldsmith's *Now*).

Research at Ashridge Management College[3] found that 75 per cent of organisations were prompted to change reactively because of financial reasons, loss of market share or recession. Only 25 per cent managed change in a proactive way prompted by a consideration of future threats and opportunities and advances in technology. Marlboro Friday is, perhaps, one of the best examples of what happens when change isn't managed proactively – Marlboro allowed its market share to slip away and then finally took action which appeared desperate rather than calculating.

Organisations may see that the world has changed but appear immune to the logical conclusion that they too must change. Often they espouse the virtues of change and the need for change, but rarely does it inculcate an organisation. The way companies are organised is the most striking example of this phenomenon.

Organisations have traditionally been viewed as vertical structures. Though organisations have tried many different ways of representing their structure most, if not all, end up with some sort of vertical axis from top to bottom. It is a striking truth that today's organisations remain modelled on the principles described by Adam Smith in 1776.

Functional organisations

Smith's concepts were re-invented for the twentieth century by Henry Ford. His legacy of strict functional organisations largely remains. In the organisation of the 1990s, there are still a vast number of controllers, overseers and supervisors. Middle managers, planners and accountants have established themselves as middle men between technology and implementation. Technology, brought in to reduce complexity, has more often than not brought with it teams of managers each intent on finding or creating their own place in the corporate order.

Hierarchies have expanded and new layers have been added with each technological step forward, note the growth of IT departments, strategy departments and so on. At one point, British Steel had an organisation chart which was so large and complex (and impractical) that it could stretch across a modestly sized office. Companies have preoccupied themselves with bridging the gap between management and workers or organising the workforce to perform more efficiently. Little attention has been paid to the role of customers, the layers of management or the core processes which enable the business to attract and retain customers.

Over the last 20 years great strides have been made in eradicating functional approaches from the factory floor. Management demarcations have, however, usually emerged unscathed. The Procter & Gamble system of brand management remains in place in a great many organisations.

Sceptics might argue that the functional system works. For over half a century brands have been managed through a period of unparalleled growth. Undoubtedly, this is true. Companies have been organised along functional lines throughout the twentieth century. They have not failed, but they have worked inefficiently. The functional system isn't broken, but it needs fixing.

Drawbacks of a functional approach

The central problems of a functional approach to brand management are detailed below.

Internal tensions: The traditional organisation is beset by tensions between different departments, systems, styles and people. Those tensions are often regarded as productive, a means of keeping people alert. But, in reality, their effect is usually negative. Functional organisation thrives on internal machinations.

The brand-oriented organisation genuinely involves people in working together fruitfully and continuously.

Goal setting: Functional organisations set goals that are functional rather than business-oriented. This means that groups of people in different functions have their own alternative targets and *raison d'être*. There may be overall corporate strategies and objectives, but they are effectively relegated in importance. A manager working in a functional organisation first and foremost requires that his or her function succeeds. Performance bonuses are usually related to divisional performance and managers are well aware that functions which succeed attract resources and the most talented people.

The end result of this is that the performance of different functions within the same organisation is often desperately uneven. Brilliant brand management may be completely negated by a slow moving R&D department unable to come up with new products as quickly as competitors.

The brand-oriented organisation sets goals which are universally generated and agreed by those they rely on to carry them through.

Job definitions: People's activities are restricted to a particular function. They are overly specialised and unable or unwilling to communicate with people elsewhere in the organisation. The brand management department has little appreciation of the concerns of people in other departments. Instead of maximising the potential of people, functional organisation denies it. As a result, people become bored and frustrated, leading to higher staff turnover. Job definitions strongly reflect the functional nature of the organisation. There are few jobs, apart from chief executive, which bridge the gap between different functions (and the chief executive may well have a specialised functional background). Job titles are unlikely to include the word 'customer' in them. Those that do are vested with little in the way of power or seniority.

The brand-oriented organisation has few job descriptions and all jobs defy conventional categorisation by function.

Responsibility: In functional organisations the customer is not the responsibility of any one person. Problems or customer queries spanning more than one department are passed on and on. Alternatively, problems are identified in purely functional terms – there is a problem with sales or an accounting problem. Identified in functional isolation they are solved in a similar style.

In the brand-oriented organisation problems are shared. Colleagues and suppliers are resources.

Communication: The functional organisation is often characterised by Byzantine communication chains. Paper passes back and forth between departments. Delays are inevitable as in-trays become more full and customers more irate. The entire process is time-consuming and inflexible. Customers are kept waiting – at Bell Atlantic a 15 to 30 day order-to-delivery cycle contained a mere 10 to 15 hours of actual work. The rest of the time was spent in waiting or was simply wasted as one department passed paperwork on to another. Similarly, at AT&T a design cycle included 80 'hand-offs' from one department to another and 24 meetings. This was later reduced to 17 and one respectively.

In the brand-oriented organisation brands are built round internal and external communication.

Self-perpetuation: As new functions and divisions are added to the basic functional structure, the old ones are never replaced. A company may have functional divisions as well as brand and product divisions and, quite possibly, geographic, national, strategic and market-driven splits between different activities. The functional organisation expands quite naturally without developing or improving.

The brand-oriented organisation re-invents itself, its business and its brands continually.

Functional gridlock

There is nothing new in revealing the inadequacies and limitations of vertical and functional structures. They have been recognised for a number of years, but attempts at breaking them down have tended to be isolated and short-term. Companies have turned to temporary project teams, task forces and various alternative matrices at times of crisis or to tackle specific localised problems. Once the problem was solved, they resorted to their old ways, continuing to gloss over the fundamental problem.

Functional organisations inevitably produce functional solutions to their problems. Functional organisations produce functional managers. Brand managers produce brand management solutions, rather than organisational solutions. 'The art of management is to promote people without making them managers', Microsoft founder Bill Gates has observed, meaning that managers become hidebound by **managing** things rather than getting them done.

If a company is patently struggling, different functional heads will advocate different functional-based solutions to the problem. The marketing director will argue that the company needs to increase its investment in marketing. If only they had more sales people making direct contact with customers they would be better able to give customers what they want. They might also suggest that the sales team would feel more confident if it had a new glossy brochure to hand to prospective customers.

The finance director is liable to shake his or her head at this point. From their point of view, the company's troubles are cost-related. If the company reduced costs it would be leaner and fitter. The production director will, in turn, argue the case for investment in better quality, more modern machinery. The chief executive, beset by arguing factions who are unlikely ever to agree, is likely to strike a balance, giving a little bit more money to each function or coming up with a company-wide initiative which each function will interpret as they wish and then ignore.

In his book *Administrative Behaviour*, Herbert Simon summed up this process and coined a phrase for it – 'satisficing' which he defined as settling for adequate instead of optimal solutions. This is an in-built characteristic of the conventional functional organisation. Past strategy is fused with current organisational culture, so that people begin to believe that they know how things are done and stop questioning the assumptions behind their thoughts and actions. The recipe for success takes over and doubts about the company's ability to actually deliver success are automatically repressed.

Companies can now afford to treat nothing as sacred and any process, resource or idea that stands in the way of satisfying the customer has to be eliminated. Instead of accepting certain tasks as inevitable, managers need to ask why they are doing a particular task so they can dispense with work that does not contribute to goals, or simply does not need to be done.

The death of the marketing function?

The 1980s were the apotheosis of marketing. Budgets expanded as surely as the self-esteem of those in marketing. Marketing became respectable and professional. Children didn't suddenly stop wanting to become astronauts to announce an interest in pursuing a career in marketing, but marketing seemed exciting and important. Unquestionably marketing is important. But in the 1980s the end result was often that companies were **marketing-driven** rather than **market-driven**. Today, the onus must be on becoming closer and more attuned and more responsive to markets.

In expanding their role during the 1980s, marketing departments moved away from their traditional focus and assumed responsibility for activities better delegated to other functions or even dispensed with altogether. They were responsible for the development of advertising, but not for the strategy behind it. Marketing in many organisations became decorative; an expensive input with an elusive and rarely measured output.

'The situation has been exacerbated by the extent to which marketing functions fail to reflect marketing as a process', says Robert Smith, one of the authors of a Coopers & Lybrand report *Marketing at the Crossroads.*

> *'Although the marketing department is usually responsible for identifying the market and creating customer profiles, it is the sales department which handles the process of generating new and repeat orders; the accounts department controls invoicing and payment; while the engineering and maintenance department deals with complaints, returned products, repairs and so forth.'*

Harvard Business School's Benson Shapiro argues that truly market-driven companies have three characteristics:

- Information on all important buying influences permeates every corporate function.
- Strategic and tactical decisions are made inter-functionally and inter-divisionally.
- Divisions and functions make well co-ordinated decisions and execute them with a sense of commitment.[4]

Thinking horizontally

The brand is where marketing meets reality. Yet, within organisations brands have often lived a charmed but isolated life. In many cases the company's top brand has little to do with the rest of the organisation. Instead it is carefully cosseted and protected by a small group of brand managers who know best. As a result, the full potential of the brand goes unfulfilled. In a group with a number of brands, functional management often keeps their individual management structures separate. As a result, synergies and economies have been overlooked.

Managing the brand should mean that the organisation adds value to the brand and that the brand adds value to the organisation. Traditionally the concentration has been on the first element. Take PepsiCo, for example. The company owns Pepsi in its various manifestations, Pizza Hut, KFC (the rather unfriendly acronym which has replaced Kentucky Fried Chicken), Taco Bell and, somewhat incongruously, Walker's Crisps. Pepsi has traditionally treated its business as autonomous units – it has concentrated on adding value to the brand. Now, it is recognising that there is a huge amount of potential overlap between its various brands.

In Pepsi's case the problem is almost that the brands are so strong they appear untouchable. Basic economies of scale were missed. It did not, for example, automatically integrate its purchasing when a new brand was acquired. As a result, each business carried on buying basic supplies (cardboard, oil, salt, etc.) and advertising separately. Pepsi estimated that savings could reach $100 million as a result of more efficient and organised purchasing.

To discover the real power of brands requires that the traditional vertical top-down axis of power be eliminated. Instead, brands and other activities need to be seen as horizontal processes. Traditional hierarchies fall away under the burden of self-examination. Rather than needing an entire office to house a complex organisational chart, layers are sparse. The American retail chain Wal-Mart, for example, has a mere three layers in its hierarchy to support a turnover in excess of $30 billion.

Of course, the elimination of hierarchies has been a notable trend of the early 1990s. Huge swathes have been cut through traditional middle management. Organisations throughout the world are restructuring or introducing labour-saving technology. Often the redundancies appear to be cases of organisations taking an indiscriminate swipe at a monster of their own creation. If an organisation can make 10 per cent of its managers redundant what have they been doing throughout all their years of employment? How well does the organisation truly understand the skills they dispense with? There are many companies where layers of hierarchy have been removed to leave a reconstituted vertical hierarchy. There are less people, but the organisational ground rules remain the same. In time, it is likely that the layers of management will return.

Achieving real change

To achieve real change, organisations need to take on new shapes. The emphasis must be on managing brands through networks rather than from a centralised brand management function at headquarters. In their book, *Collaborating to Compete*, McKinsey consultants Joel Bleeke and David Ernst predict:

> *'Global corporations of the future will be rather like amoebas. The amoeba is always changing shape, taking and giving with the surroundings, yet it always retains its integrity and identity as a unique creature.'*[5]

The organisation shape of the future is most persuasively laid out by the UK management thinker Charles Handy.

> *'The micro-division of labour has fostered a basic distrust of human beings. People weren't allowed to put the whole puzzle together. Instead they were given small parts because companies feared what people would do if they knew and saw the whole puzzle'*,

says Handy. 'Human assets shouldn't be misused. Brains are becoming the core of organisations – other activities can be contracted out.' He points to Singapore which has largely exported its manufacturing activities elsewhere, but retains managerial control.

Handy foresees a world in which half as many people will be paid twice as much to do three times as much work. For managers, says Handy, this will involve a fundamental shift in emphasis. 'Managers have been brought up on a diet of power, divide and rule. They have been preoccupied with authority rather than making things happen.' His image of the organisation of the future has evolved from a shamrock in his book, *The Age of Unreason* ('a form of organisation based around a core of essential executives and workers supported by outside contractors and part-time help') to the 'doughnut principle' of his most recent book, *The Empty Raincoat* ('Organisations have their essential core of jobs and people surrounded by an open and flexible space which they fill with flexible workers and flexible supply contracts'). Handy argues that organisations have neglected and misunderstood the core while expanding and developing the rest of the doughnut. He attaches the same image to people's personal development, suggesting that many need to sit down and return to first principles if they are to achieve a balance in their lives.

The 'federal' organisation is something which Handy continues to champion: 'an old idea whose time may have come'. Through federalism Handy believes the modern company can bridge some of the paradoxes it continually faces, such as the need to be simultaneously global and local. 'Every organisation can be thought of in federal terms,' he says, adding the challenge: 'Federalism is an exercise in the balancing of power.' Handy accepts that federalism is often neither clear-cut nor easy to implement, indeed it is often nebulous and on the verge of being out of control.

Such ideas strike at the heart of the functional organisation. The shape of organisations is already changing. The way in which brands are managed within these organisations is also set to change in dramatic ways and, in some cases, is already doing so.

Brands as virtual projects

The physical manifestation of a company once centred around the office. Technology now enables organisations to provide a more dynamic and flexible approach to the traditional office and how people work within it. Indeed, the office may cease to exist as work is undertaken elsewhere and the organisation becomes increasingly diffuse and intangible: the virtual organisation.

'In the 1990s and beyond, the smart organisation is the one that survives', says Laurence Lyons, consultant and part of Henley Management College's Future Work Forum. Lyons points to the existence of virtual competitors as well as virtual organisations.

'Another important, yet different form, is the stealthy transparent

competitor – to be found on the other side of the coin to the virtual competitor. The term "virtual" means that it is apparent, although the substance seems intangible. There is absolutely no doubt, on the other hand, that "transparent" organisations exist in substance, yet cannot easily be seen. That is until they surface, when they become highly visible and very real indeed.'

Virtual competitors emerge from nowhere. 'Think for a moment about what business General Motors is in? Obviously it makes millions of vehicles. But, today, it is also in the credit card business', says Laurence Lyons.

He also points to the Dana Corporation which is in the automotive business, but one of its outstanding divisions is in commercial credit, running leasing programmes for computer companies such as Apple and Compaq. Its typical customer leases only one or two systems, yet Dana has turned this into a highly profitable business.

It is into this virtual world that brands must be transported if they are to survive and thrive. Key to this will be the effective use of a more traditional management tool – project management in unconventional ways.

Projects were once easily defined one-offs, like building a bridge. Now, the essence of brand management is likely to be project-based. Instead of being neatly compartmentalised under the all-embracing title of brand management, the management and organisation of brands will move dynamically throughout the organisation.

Figure 12.1 shows what a functional organisation may have looked like in the past.

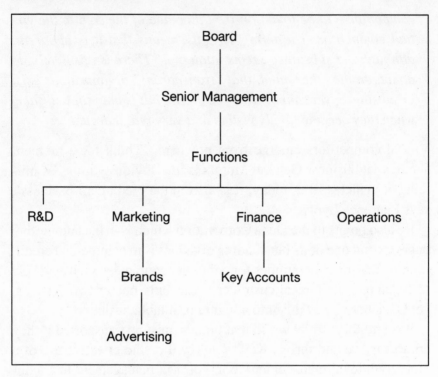

Figure 12.1 Conventional functional organisation

In contrast the new organisation is built round free-flowing combinations (see Figure 12.2).

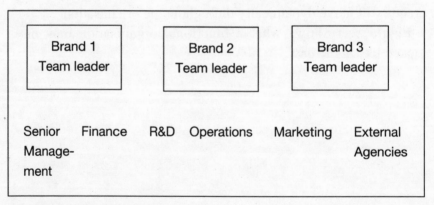

Figure 12.2 New organisation

Expertise is brought in and out of the teams as required, rather than sitting unused within them.

Characteristics of project-based brand management

Such systems rely on a number of vital elements all of which require substantial changes in organisation and the skills of individuals, as follows.

Giving responsibility

If brands are to be accepted as having value which is highly important to future corporate success the responsibility for brands must be taken at a higher level of management than ever before. Also, the organisation must be geared to making brands work successfully. This requires that brands – their development and management – are not simply a function but the overall responsibility of everyone in the organisation.

Companies like McDonald's and British Airways have realised that the development of the brand must be led from the top, but equally that it is the responsibility of everyone in the organisation. Poor service by an individual counts against the brand as a whole.

The functional organisation has difficulty in making such links. Responsibility is granted and does not move. Poor service is regarded as a local issue, the responsibility of the supervisor to sort out.

If functional thinking is to be eradicated and everyone in an organisation is to take their share of responsibility for the brand then true responsibility must be delegated.

Comparisons may be drawn with the quality gurus Deming and Juran who have championed quality as the responsibility of everyone. They argue that if people are given the tools and techniques to check their own work then inspection by quality controllers is all but eliminated and people have a far greater sense of pride in their work. In contrast, Deming argues that leaving responsibility for quality to an inspector at the end of the procedure simply leads to the fault multiplying and linking with others. The result is a costly high percentage of rejected products. In an example, cited by Deming, RCA sought to maximise its profits by using cheaper and inferior parts in its televisions. As a result, more sets broke down while under guarantee and many proved too expensive to repair and had to be discarded and expensively replaced by the company.

American insurance company, Aetna Life and Casualty, has granted substantial autonomy to its sales force. The old hierarchy of supervisors and agents has been replaced by work teams of around 17 people. Aetna has completely overhauled the business of issuing a policy. In 1992 it had 22 business centres with a staff of 3,000. It took around 15 days to get a basic policy out of the office. Now, the operation has been reduced to 700 employees in four centres. Customers receive their policies within five days. A single person sitting at a networked PC can perform all the necessary steps to process an application immediately. It is estimated that the new system for issuing policies will save $40 million and improve productivity by 25 per cent.

Building brands through teams

Teamworking, like empowerment, has been pushed to the forefront of managerial minds in the last decade. The two are closely linked. Both, however, have usually been interpreted as a tool for use only on the factory floor or in creative service businesses such as advertising. By and large, managers have been passed by.

If brands are to be fully developed, teamworking needs to be introduced throughout an organisation so that multi-skilled teams become permanently established and involve everyone. Some may involve customers and suppliers.

Graeme Leith of Sundridge Park defines a team as

'two or more people working for a common goal for which they hold themselves mutually accountable. Teamwork is achieving the more successful completion of a task by working together, than the separate individuals would have done by working alone'.

He says that most teams can be classified in one of three ways:

- Teams that make recommendations.
- Teams that make or do things.
- Teams that run things.

Teams can be internal (within a department, across departments) or, as they are increasingly, external (with suppliers or customers). Wherever they are found, successful teamwork is based upon three fundamentals for each team member:

- Esteem
- Trust
- Confidence.

An example of the level of teamworking involved can be seen at the German company Bosch. At its new plant in Eisenach, eastern Germany, product line teams are given responsibility for the entire process covered by the line from suppliers to clients. People in the line team are broken down into teams of between 10 and 15 people. The factory's rewards policy is tightly linked to team performance and wages include a team premium for the team's performance as well as elements tied to the views of other team members on an individual's performance.

One company tackling the issue is Elida Gibbs, the UK personal products subsidiary of Unilever. Its brands include Fabergé, Brut, Pears, Signal and Timotei. In a revolutionary move, Elida Gibbs abolished the post of brand manager and re-invented the sales team as the 'customer development process'. Brands are now the responsibility of brand development managers.

The changes at Elida Gibbs stem from criticisms of its performance in the late-1980s. Poor delivery standards and an old-fashioned ordering system were a source of irritation to customers. As a result, Elida Gibbs introduced teamworking at one of its factories in 1988. Responsibility for each production line was transferred to those working on it. As well as these changes, Elida Gibbs reduced the number of its suppliers and gave suppliers more responsibility for quality control, testing and development. The roles of the company's managers were also redefined on the basis of processes. Functional divisions were replaced by 'seamless teams'. Many of the day-to-day contacts with retailers which used up brand managers' time have been passed on to customer development managers.

Over the last three years change-over time on one production line has been reduced to less than four hours, when it previously took an entire day. In addition, 90 per cent of orders are now correctly completed, against 72 per cent in the past. Between 1989 and 1991 the company's pre-tax profits rose by 73 per cent and margins widened from 6.5 per cent to 10 per cent. In April 1993 Elida Gibbs launched its first major product since its internal changes. This involved a development process of less than six months, half as much time as development had previously taken.

Similarly, SmithKline Beecham spent much of 1993 overhauling its marketing activities. It believed it had been hampered by the company being divided into geographic units. SmithKline Beecham studied other companies, including Procter & Gamble and Unilever, and then set up six teams each responsible for a product category. The teams were given a free rein to co-opt managers from national subsidiaries. Sales in consumer brands rose by 11 per cent in 1993 and product development cycles have been accelerated – a new toothbrush was developed in 40 per cent of the previous time.

Limitations of teamworking

Though teamworking has attracted a great deal of recent attention, it is worth noting that teamworking does not, in itself, bring an organisation closer to customers. Indeed, research by consultant and author, Colin Coulson-Thomas, involving more than 100 organisations, concluded that teamworking was often failing to deliver quality and other performance improvements. 'There is a danger that groups or teams are focusing excessively on internal dynamics at the expense of external customers', warned Coulson-Thomas.[6] Teams are an essential factor in nurturing brands and in achieving change initiatives, but not an all-embracing automatic solution. They, too, can lead to the sort of demarcations which so weaken functional approaches to business organisation.

Indeed, despite all the theorising about teams and teamworking the basic dynamics of teamworking often remain clouded and uncertain. Teams only occur when a number of people have a common goal and recognise that their personal success is dependent on the success of others. They are all interdependent. In practice, this means that in most teams people will contribute individual skills, many of which will be different. It also means that the full tensions and counterbalance of human behaviour will need to be demonstrated in the team.

It is not enough to have a rag-bag collection of individual skills. The various behaviours of the team members need to mesh together in order to achieve objectives. For people to work well together you need both a range of specific skills or technical skills and a range of different human behaviours. When you look hard at people and how they behave when they are working in teams you find that in addition to the actual content of the work they are doing, they take on certain behaviours. Each person has a favourite way of behaving when they work with others.

Modern management thinking suggests that you need a balance of behaviours for any change in management activity. But you may wish to slightly unbalance the team in favour of the type of change you are trying to undertake.

Teams remain a law unto themselves. Managers who sit down and play at human engineering by trying to select exactly the right sort of combination usually end up in a state of confusion. Often teams which prove to be effective come about spontaneously or include an unusual combination of specialists. The key to success does not appear to lie in the selection of team members, you only have to look briefly at team sports to find examples of talented individuals working poorly as a team. Instead, success is often characterised by the genuine granting of power and responsibility to teams so they can solve their own problems.

Notes

1   Pascale, R., quoted in 'Turning doers back into thinkers', *Independent on Sunday*, 28 November 1993.
2   Davidow, W., & Malone, M., *The Virtual Corporation*, Harper Collins, New York, 1992.
3   Ashridge Management Research Group, *Triggers for Change*, AMRG, 1989.
4   Shapiro, B., 'What the hell is market oriented?', *Harvard Business Review*, November–December 1988.
5   Bleeke, J., & Ernst, D., *Collaborating to Compete*, John Wiley, New York, 1993.
6   Coulson-Thomas, C., *Harnessing the Potential of Groups*, Lotus Development, 1993.

13

NEW SKILLS FOR BRAND MANAGEMENT

THE END OF SPECIALISM

In the traditional organisation the brand manager was an intermediary rather than an active participant. Information, decisions and data was disseminated by the brand manager rather than acted on. This was reflected in the people who held brand management jobs. Often, brand management was seen as something you did early in your career for a short period before moving on to more general and 'demanding' management tasks.

In a damning indictment, John Murphy, chairman of Interbrand, has commented:

'The concept of the brand manager in most companies is that the manager isn't managing anything. The brand manager is merely a link between the company and the ad agency. A manager in this country is somebody who has been out of university for two or three years, joined the company as a trainee, did a couple of years repping, selling sanitary towels in Aberystwyth and was considered to be quite bright and lively and was brought in and put in charge of a brand and given no data. He was given no seniority and no real ability to make decisions and in most companies he just ended up as a link person, not really managing a brand at all and in no way accountable for the financial performance of the brand. I've nothing against brand managers. I just think the brand management function should be doing a totally different and much more senior job than it is currently

doing in this country. I think we need a fundamental reappraisal of the role of brand management in this country. It's happening in a few companies now; where the brand managers are being seen in a more senior and more potent role, but there is still a long way to go.[1]

In the organisation of the future jobs are likely to be multi-dimensional. This does not apply only to factory floor workers, but to everyone in the organisation.

Traditionally the job of the brand manager was built around the following:

- **Information gathering:** interpreting and generating information on products and performance.

- **Measurement:** calculating brand awareness, details of particular markets, consumer preferences and trends etc. and then analysing the results.

- **Planning:** playing a part in setting targets for the brand in annual planning and budgetary cycles.

- **Implementation:** making the plan happen.

Already the days of the specialist are numbered:

- At IBM Credit four types of specialist have been replaced by a single, multi-skilled 'deal structurer', who calls upon a small central pool of specialist back-up staff when needed.

- Microsoft has 15 grades of management. At its top are seven people known as the 'architects'. They involve themselves in any projects which require attention and then evaluate the issues at stake. They are the people who the company's chief executive, Bill Gates, works with and through whom he communicates his ideas to the rest of the organisation.

- At AT&T multi-functional 'design cells' handle each project from customer request to delivery. This previously involved specialists in five different departments.

- At Bell Atlantic a 'case team' carries out previously separate tasks.

Multi-skilled and flexible, the new brand manager will no longer be a cipher. 'The task of the brand manager is still to generate profits in the short term and to build brand equity to ensure profits in the long term', say Chris Styles and Tim Ambler of London Business School.

'The focus of managerial activity is the improvement of relationships within the network from the perspective of the brand. The brand manager essentially becomes a network or relationship manager.'

THE NEW SKILLS

If the very nature of brand management is to change, this clearly requires flexible and variable inputs from people. Brand managers, and others, lose the security of job specialisms and set procedures, while managers suddenly find their performance under closer scrutiny. Managers can no longer fall back on functional hierarchies or traditional ways of doing things to protect themselves. What they do and how they work is stripped bare for all to see.

The key skills for the future are:

- Managing contention.
- Managing ambiguity.
- Managing people.
- Managing projects.
- Flexibility and leadership.
- Managing strategy.
- Managing their own development.

Managing contention

Managers are generally unused to rigorous and ceaseless questioning. Often they are extremely uncomfortable with the idea of their work being analysed in anything other than a superficial way. The potential for dissension and conflict is high.

If, for example, a team is made up of an engineer, a customer development manager and a company accountant, some sort of conflict is inevitable, and often healthy. There are and will be basic misunderstandings. The manager might ask the engineer why he is doing something in a certain way. Reared on a diet of functional division, the engineer may well say that he has always done it that way and he knows more about engineering than the manager. To make teams work, however, mutual respect must exist or be developed. Managers have to learn to accept objective input from people they regard as outsiders.

Author of *Managing on the Edge*, Richard Pascale estimates that 50 per cent of the time contentious issues are smoothed over and avoided. Around 30 per cent lead to non-productive fighting and no resolution while only 20 per cent are truly confronted and resolved.[2]

Harvard's Chris Argyris has examined in great depth the debilitating machinations of a firm of consultants. He found that the consultants, despite their learning and expertise, were adept at masking their errors and misjudgements. Problems were routinely bypassed and covered up, one cover-up led to another and so on. Board meetings were spent discussing peripheral issues while major issues were routinely glossed over. Argyris' conclusion is that the more threatening a problem is to those responsible for solving it the deeper it will be ingrained under layers of corporate camouflage. Argyris' cure is for organisations to start learning from the top down.

Managers, no matter how senior they are, must candidly and clearly take responsibility for their errors of judgement as well as their triumphs.

Managing ambiguity

The process of change creates a new sense of ambiguity. In turbulent times people are uncertain about their roles and unsure what they should be doing and with whom. This ambiguity covers a number of areas:

- Job definitions: changes in the scope and nature of job definitions are, for many, deeply unsettling and remove a prime reference point.

- Responsibilities: people are unsure what they are responsible for and to whom.

- Expectations: people are uncertain about what colleagues and the organisation expects from them.

An obvious adjunct to the process of ambiguity is the disappearance of career ladders. Organisations shorn of their vertical hierarchy can appear to offer little opportunity for progression. IBM UK chairman, Sir Anthony Cleaver, announced that his organisation was reducing its number of management tiers to a mere four. This, said Cleaver, 'means a maximum of one promotion every ten years and even this is for the one man who makes it to the top'.

One UK life assurance company restructured its customer servicing division. Team-based operations are now in place with three layers of management instead of the previous seven. Customer service representatives have replaced administrators and clerks and they now have a different reward and performance appraisal system. But the opportunities for promotional advancement up the career ladder no longer exist. The new approach focuses on recognition through teamwork, with managers being elected by team colleagues. Adapting to the changes requires that the employees radically realign their career expectations and measurements of success.

Those who plan to join the upwardly mobile and who still believe in neat and well-ordered career structures are increasingly likely to be disappointed. The Institute of Management (IM) tracked the career development of over 800 UK managers from 1980 to 1992. The IM found that sideways or downwards moves among managers more than doubled during that period, from 7 per 100 managers in 1980–1982 to nearly 15 per 100 in 1992.[3]

'As the pace of change accelerates, the idea of a progressive career within stable organisational structures is increasingly threatened', says the IM report based on the research. 'The structures which have traditionally supported rational long-term careers are being gradually replaced with more fluid organisations.' And it is people who are the most fluid of corporate resources.

Strangely, the insecurity has not yet transmitted itself to some managers. Trudy Coe, co-author of the survey, says: 'Managers have to be prepared and, at the moment, many appear complacent. They think their careers are safe.'

Research carried out by the IM in 1992 found that 40 per cent of managers anticipated that their next career move would be upwards. 'Managers need to look at their careers differently', says Coe.

> *'They have to see sideways moves as an opportunity to develop the broad portfolio of skills they now need. In the past managers looked to organisations to shape their careers and skills for them, now the onus is on them. They need to be prepared for change and to recognise its potential benefits rather than regarding it as a threat.'*

Managing people

Describing the skills now needed in brand management, two senior managers commented:

> *'I think they have to have a lot of the touchy-feely things you don't see in the ads, which includes multicultural sensitivity and understanding. If you haven't got that, you have major problems'.*

> *'We are finding that there are different personality attributes and maturity levels required to operate in a cross-country or cross-functional team arrangement. That requires not so much experience, as maturity. There are, after all, a lot of experienced people who are immature'.*

In the new environment brand managers change from supervisors to coaches. They are there to provide resources, answer questions and look out for the long-term development of the brand and the team. How they deal with people is key to their day-to-day success and to the progression of their career within the organisation.

Delegation

No longer is delegation an occasional managerial indulgence. Instead, it is a necessity. 'With organisations becoming flatter and hierarchies disappearing managers now have a far wider span of control than ever before', says John Payne, consultant and author of *Letting Go Without Losing Control*. 'In that situation, delegation is vital. The trouble is that delegation is like driving a car – no one admits to being a bad delegator.'

It is not only the fact that many managers consider themselves to be competent delegators that causes problems. Good delegation is hard work and requires substantial amounts of confidence and faith; managers, after all, are usually delegating tasks which they are accomplished at carrying out to less experienced people. 'Delegation is being prepared to trust people to do a task and achieve results without your interference', says John Payne.

> *'It is easier said than done. Managers who make delegation work for them are those who have eliminated fear. They do not delegate and then sit worrying that the job won't be done well enough and they will be blamed or have to sort it out. They have confidence in their own position and are not fearful that the person will do too good a job and undermine their position and authority. Also, they make time to delegate properly. Initially, delegation does involve committing time, but there are substantial time savings in the near future.'*

Unfortunately, old habits die hard. Organisations may have shrunk, but managers often remain wedded to habits of a lifetime.

> *'Many companies are in a state of transition. They have taken layers of management out but haven't yet changed the processes. The remaining managers still have a lot of pressure on them and are often working very long hours',*

says Ginny Spittle, a senior human resources manager at ICL.

> *'The role of managers is changing from controlling and planning to coaching, leading and acting as a resource. If they are to*

achieve this change they need training and support so they learn to delegate and give full responsibility to people who report to them.'

The need for training and support is one also identified by Richard Phillips of Ashridge Management College. 'Managers have to come to terms with the fact that they can no longer manage people in a hands-on way any more and dumping trivial tasks onto people is not the best way to delegate', he says.

'Managers tend to delegate tasks which they are too busy to do themselves or which they don't want to do themselves. They also tend to delegate them to staff who are judged to be already competent to carry them out to minimise the risk of mistakes and reduce the manager's anxiety levels.'

In short, delegation is a last resort, a worry to the manager doing the delegating and an unwanted extra burden to the person handed the task. But, Richard Phillips argues, it need not be like that. He has carried out extensive research on managers who act as coaches. By doing so, he says, managers turn conventional wisdom about delegation on its head.

'Instead of selecting someone who can already do the work being delegated, coaches deliberately select someone who cannot do it. In addition to setting the goals of the actual work to be done, they add learning goals. They coach the learner to give them the necessary skills and confidence to carry out the task.'

The need to combine learning, task-fulfilment and delegation is also seen as essential by ICL's Ginny Spittle:

'Managers have to look at more creative approaches. The onus is now on getting the most out of groups and teams of people, but there simply isn't the time to sit down with everyone who reports directly to you. Managers have to delegate successfully so that everyone learns and contributes as the job is done.'

Ashridge's Richard Phillips cites an example from a major electronics company he talked to as part of his research on coaching.

> *'The job of negotiating a large and important maintenance con-*
> *tract was delegated to a senior programmer. There were clear*
> *goals, learning objectives and the expectations of both sides were*
> *thoroughly aired and discussed beforehand. The end-result was*
> *that the manager new to the job learned more about his own com-*
> *pany; gained an external perspective; and developed interper-*
> *sonal and negotiating skills. Not only that – he met the target of*
> *reducing the cost of the contract by 10 per cent.'*

Of course, the once simple act of delegation has also been hijacked by management writers. Instead of delegating, managers are now 'empowering', granting new areas of responsibility. Though this is now part of the language of management, examples of empower-ment are not always what they may seem. 'With the flattening of hierarchies, empowerment has become a fashionable term. In prac-tice, it is often a synonym for delegation', warns Dr Ian Cunning-ham. Instead of granting genuine power to their staff, managers remain as likely as ever to make the important decisions and only pass on relatively unimportant tasks to others. It is worth remem-bering that empowerment and delegation are not one and the same. Delegation starts off as part of a manager's job which he or she then delegates. Empowerment, however, involves removing constraints which prevent someone doing their job as effectively as possible.

The danger is that while empowerment attracts the management theorists and fad-following companies, delegation remains neglected, its full potential unrealised. A persuasive argument to sit up and take notice comes from Richard Phillips: 'Managers should remember that when they perform a task which someone else could do, they prevent themself from doing a task which only they could do.'

Managing projects

According to project management guru Eddie Obeng, today's pro-ject manager (more accurately referred to as a project leader) needs training in four key areas:

- Planning and controlling: project leaders need to be able to use a variety of methods to ensure they are keeping on schedule and within budget. Even more important, they need to be able to decide priorities for their objectives.

- Learning skills: as most project leaders are working in an unfamiliar context it is crucial that they assimilate knowledge as rapidly as possible. This will enable them to adjust their plans and objectives and save valuable time and money. To do this, project leaders need to keep learning, planning, reviewing and changing.

- People skills: project leaders need to be able to negotiate for vital resources; be able to influence people to gain their commitment; be able to listen, to co-ordinate and control the project; and be able to manage stakeholders from throughout the business.

- Organisational skills: project leaders need to be politically astute and aware of the potential impact of wider organisational issues. They should be adept at networking with senior employees, should understand how the organisation works, and should have a larger picture of the organisation's goals and necessary conditions.

Flexibility and leadership

Leadership and flexibility were once mutually incompatible. But a horizontal cross-functional and team-based environment requires a flexible style of managing, with the manager sometimes giving firm directions in order to ensure that the process output conforms to customer expectations, while at other times stepping back and allowing team members to take decisions.

'The leader's role has changed. It has become more complex and arguably even more critical to success', says Peter Phillips, head of leadership programmes at BP.

'Leaders must ensure that high performance levels are achieved and sustained; handle complexity and ambiguity; enjoy leading

*the change process; ensure that the organisation and its pro-
cesses constantly develop; and that people within the company
are motivated, developed and rewarded to produce outstanding
results.'*

The new business leaders have to be veritable Renaissance men and
women. To help develop its leaders, BP has a leadership compe-
tency model and development framework. But is this too structured
a means of identifying and nurturing tomorrow's leaders? Peter
Phillips contends that any system must be able to cope with individualism:

*'Individuality, flexibility and scope for mavericks must be
retained. The purpose of the development framework is to identify
and develop the leaders who will deliver performance today and
in the future. The aim is to let talent develop and flourish not to
clone leaders'.*

The very individualism associated with leadership is also now a
bone of contention. The people we tend to think of as leaders, from
Napoleon to Margaret Thatcher, are not exactly renowned for their
teamworking skills. But these are exactly the skills which are all-
important for managing brands in the 1990s and beyond.

'In some cases, the needs of a situation bring to the fore individuals with unique qualities or values, however, most leaders have to fit
their skills, experience and vision to a particular time and place',
says psychologist Robert Sharrock of YSC.

*'Today's leaders have to be pragmatic and flexible to survive.
Increasingly, this means being people rather than task-oriented.
The "great man" theory about leadership rarely applies – if
teams are what make businesses run, then we have to look beyond
individual leaders to groups of people with a variety of leadership
skills.'*

Indeed, the pendulum has swung so far that there is growing interest
in the study of followers. Once the humble foot soldier was ignored
as commentators sought out the General, now the foot soldiers are

encouraged to voice their opinions and shape how the organisation works.

> *'Followers are becoming more powerful. It is now common for the performance of bosses to be scrutinised and appraised by their corporate followers. This, of course, means that leaders have to actively seek the support of their followers in a way they would have never have previously contemplated',*

says Robert Sharrock.

Phil Hodgson of Ashridge Management College has analysed a number of business leaders. His conclusion is the old models of leadership are no longer appropriate.

> *'Generally, the managers had outgrown the notion of the individualistic leader. Instead, they regarded leadership as a question of drawing people and disparate parts of the organisation together in a way that made individuals and the organisation more effective.'*

He concludes that the new leader must add value as a coach, mentor and problem solver; allow people to accept credit for success and responsibility for failure; and must continually evaluate and enhance their own leadership role. 'They don't follow rigid or orthodox role models, but prefer to nurture their own unique leadership style', he says. 'And, they don't do people's jobs for them or put their faith in developing a personality cult.' The new recipe for leadership, says Hodgson, centres on five key areas: learning, energy, simplicity, focus and inner sense.

In contrast, traditional views of leadership tend eventually to concentrate on vision and charisma. The message seems to be that charisma is no longer enough to carry leaders through – leaders with strong personalities are as likely as others to bite the corporate dust (as Bob Horton found to his cost at BP). The new model leaders include people like Percy Barnevik at Asea Brown Boveri, Virgin's Richard Branson and Jack Welch at GE in the United States.

The magic which marks them apart has been analysed by INSEAD leadership expert Manfred Kets de Vries. 'They go beyond narrow definitions. They have an ability to excite people in their organisations', he says.

'They also work extremely hard – leading by example is not dead – and are highly resistant to stress. Also, leaders like Branson or Barnevik are very aware of what their failings are. They make sure that they find good people who can fill these areas.'

In the age of empowerment, the ability to delegate effectively is critically important.

'Empowerment and leadership are not mutually exclusive',

says Professor de Vries.

'The trouble is that many executives feel it is good to have control. They become addicted to power – and that is what kills companies.'

Managing strategy

Michael Birkin, chief executive of Interbrand has predicted:

'Despite publicity concerning the pressure brands are under, our view is that strong brands will continue to play a key role in the shopping basket. They will be as relevant in five or ten years' time as they were five or ten years ago. Those with no clear plans will struggle.'

From being a strictly operational issue, brand management is now a strategic issue. Brand managers cannot solely be concerned with the nitty gritty of direct implementation. Managers need also to understand how day-to-day brand management aligns with strategic goals and performance measures.

Recalling how brand man-

> **Strong brands will continue to play a key role in the shopping basket. They will be as relevant in five or ten years' time as they were five or ten years ago.**

agement was handled traditionally in his company, Elida Gibbs chairman Helmut Ganser has said:

> 'The brand manager was looking at new brands. But at the same time he was supposed to run short-term practical promotions with trade customers, with a completely different time perspective. And if you have short-term pressures, you know which one takes precedence.'[4]

This change requires that brand managers have, for example, an understanding of the company's mission, competitive capabilities and core stakeholders. They must fully understand and communicate overall strategy to achieve the elimination of non-value adding activities, the enhancement of value adding activities, gains in productivity and far greater market responsiveness.

'Launching, building, supporting and leveraging brand assets takes a different set of skills than managing a product line', says H. David Hennessey of the US's Babson College.

> 'A long-term strategic view is needed of how the company should use its assets to manage the brand identity in the mind of the consumer. The traditional tactical decisions of product, price, trade promotions and communications plans need to be made in the context of their impact on the value of the brand assets. Finally, in many cases the role of domestic versus global branding must be questioned. If such factors are overlooked or a short-term perspective is taken organisations will dilute the value of their brands and, ultimately, their own value.'

The problem is that in an era of constant and unpredictable change, the practical usefulness of strategy is being increasingly, and loudly, questioned. The sceptics argue that it is all well and good to come up with a brilliantly formulated strategy, but quite another to implement it. By the time implementation begins, the business environment is liable to have changed and be in the process of changing even further.

Some well-known names are among those sounding the death knell for traditional approaches to strategy. In his book *The Rise and*

Fall of Strategic Planning Henry Mintzberg takes on the full might of conventional planning orthodoxy. 'Too much analysis gets in our way. The failure of strategic planning is the failure of formalisation', says Mintzberg, identifying formalisation as the fatal flaw of modern management.

Mintzberg argues the case for, what he labels, 'strategic programming'. His view is that strategy has for too long been housed in ivory towers built from corporate data and analysis. It has become distant from reality, when to have any viable commercial life strategy needs to become completely immersed in reality. 'Strategies appear at predetermined times, popping out when expected, full blown, all ready for implementation. It is almost as if they are immaculately conceived', he caustically observes.

While the debate rages, the fundamental questions posed in the formulation of strategy remain as valid now as ever, probably more so. Strategy seeks to establish which type of customers organisations want. It drives them to consider and identify their competitive edge, and moves them to consider the sort of organisation they want to be.

None of these issues is readily resolved. But it is overly pessimistic to believe that they **cannot** be resolved (or to hark back to imaginary times when the answers appeared effortlessly).

The way forward

The starting point to moving nearer towards solutions, and the implementation of strategy, must be a solid understanding of where you are starting from and the dilemmas you face. If organisations are not in touch with the reality of their situation (however depressing this may seem) they have no hope of moving forward.

They must also be aware that, as they move forward, they are not going to do so in a straight unswerving line. In the 1960s and 1970s, when 'Management by Objectives' was popular, organisations could chart a course from A to B. Today, they may chart the course, but will find that it is not direct. The important ability now is to be able to hold on to a general direction rather than to slavishly follow a predetermined path.

Such flexibility demands a broader perspective of the organisation's activities and direction. There needs to be stronger awareness of the links between strategy, change, teamworking and learning. In particular, the ability to transmit learning across and through the organisation is key to implementing strategy in the 1990s.

The new emphasis is on the **process** of strategy as well as the output. Strategy is as essential today as it ever was, but now it needs to include brands at all stages in its formulation and implementation.

Managing their own development

To meet the new challenge requires managers to think beyond position and develop comprehensive general skills which will allow them to respond flexibly to organisational needs. It is not surprising, therefore, that people at all levels in organisations are seeing the opportunities for personal development. Indeed, it is increasingly regarded as a major part of what was once called the remuneration package.

When it came to management development, managers were often pawns in the hands of the organisation. If the company thought a manager needed a particular skill they were speedily despatched on a suitable course. As their careers progressed, managers assembled an impressive list of courses they had attended though what they actually learned was often infrequently measured.

In some companies development is still regarded in these terms. However, the skills needed by managers in the 1990s are so wide-ranging that picking off skills is no longer enough. Managers and their organisations have to be more selective and focused when it comes to development.

As part of this growing trend, managers, and their companies, now realise that developing managerial skills and techniques is not simply the responsibility of the company. Managers, too, have a role to play in being proactive and identifying areas in which they need to develop. Today, instead of being pawns moved around by corporate might, managers are increasingly encouraged to examine their own strengths and weaknesses to develop the skills necessary for the future. Rather than having their development mapped out for them, managers are managing it for themselves.

LEADING BRANDS FROM THE TOP

Despite the protestations of annual reports, senior managers are often the strongest and most persuasive corporate force against the process of change. Though they may appreciate brands as assets in their annual report, they have a tendency to take them less seriously in practice. They are, after all, creatures of the functional organisation – some will have spent their entire careers working within a particular culture in a particular way. As a result, they are protective of their own sphere of influence, often unwilling to upset the corporate equilibrium and unlikely to become passionate advocates of any one idea. They are in favour of stability and more of the same – it has elevated them to the corporate heights.

In the 1990s, such conservatism or plain stagnation is a guarantee of failure. 'If the top is committed deeply to maintaining the status quo, there's no hope', says P. Ranganath Nayak, senior vice-president of consultants Arthur D. Little.

Author and change management expert, Dr Ian Cunningham says:

'The old planning models are no longer enough. You cannot plan for a revolution. Instead, companies and managers need to prepare; managers need to be quicker, more able and feel confident enough to buck trends and be different. While it is difficult for many managers to develop this ability, they have to remember that you make money by not going along with the market. When it comes to change management, managers no longer have the luxury of being able to learn from their mistakes. They have to get it right.'

Senior managers must become visionaries for the brands they manage. Their visions cannot be static or unachievable. Constant change in markets and technology means that a company's destination is also likely to be constantly changing. In General Electric's

1990 annual report, chief executive Jack Welch mapped out the company's vision: 'Our dream for the 1990s is a boundaryless company ... where we knock down the walls that separate us from each other on the inside and from our key constituents on the outside.'

> **Senior managers must become visionaries for the brands they manage. Their visions cannot be static or unachievable.**

After initial enthusiasm for corporate visions in the 1980s, recent years have seen mounting scepticism about their real value. Often they appear overly ambitious and entirely unrelated to the current situation of the business. Senior managers must bridge the gap between the vision and the day-to-day reality.

To do so, requires constant communication of what brands and the organisation value and stand for. Research by the consulting firm, Ingersoll Engineers, cited the communication problems faced in change programmes. Communication both upwards and downwards is considered crucial. 'Frequently the downward is there, but the upward falls on deaf ears', commented one manager in the survey of top UK directors. 'Attempts [to change] without communicating....lead to the suspicion of a hidden agenda', said another. 'Communicating a clear plan superlatively well is central to creating the confidence for successful change', says Brian Small, managing director of Ingersoll.[5]

Leaders must inspire. Robert Haas, chairman and chief executive of Levi Strauss, has observed:

> *'A strategy is no good if people don't fundamentally believe in it. We had a strategy in the late 1970s and early 1980s that emphasised diversification. We acquired companies, created new brands, and applied our traditional brand to different kinds of apparel. Our people did what they were asked to do, but the problem was, they didn't believe in it.'*

Leaders must create and sustain this belief.

Notes

1 Quoted in Haigh, D., *Strategic Control of Marketing Finance*, FT/Pitman, London, 1994.
2 Pascale, R., 'The benefit of a clash of opinions', Personnel Management, October 1993.
3 Institute of Management, *Are career ladders disappearing?*, IM, 1993.
4 Quoted in 'Marketing's new model army', *Management Today*, March 1994.
5 'Putting over the message', *Financial Times*, 3 September 1993.

14

BUILDING REAL POWER

There is the perennial suspicion that actually building a successful brand is relatively easy. Given a large budget and a half decent product or service, any manager and any organisation could convert a name, package, logo and snappy advertisement into a multi-million pound money-spinner for years to come. In fact, nothing could be further from the truth. Not only is there a lengthy trail of failed brands, but those which have reached the top have to fight very hard to stay there.

There is no recipe for success, but some of the key ingredients of building a brand with real power are likely to include:

- A culture which matches the brand.
- Keeping the brand fresh.
- Building from crises.
- Using Information Technology to build brands.
- Moving closer to customers and suppliers.
- Utilising design.

A CULTURE WHICH MATCHES THE BRAND

A survey by communications consultants Smythe Dorwood Lambert interviewed 46 chief executives from leading UK companies; it found that 'attention to reputation, where image matches reality is now a commercial imperative'.

If you are a manufacturer of high precision watches and your slogan is 'Always on time', it is clearly unhelpful when developing your brand if all your organisation's activities are notoriously late.

Given a large budget and a half decent product or service, any manager and any organisation could convert a name, package, logo and snappy advertisement into a multi-million pound money-spinner for years to come. In fact, nothing could be further from the truth. Not only is there a lengthy trail of failed brands, but those which have reached the top have to fight very hard to stay there.

To a greater or lesser extent the culture of your company must be aligned to the character of your brand.

Perhaps the greatest example of this in practice is IBM and its founder Thomas Watson Senior. Few business people create companies in their own image which then thrive after their departure. Most plummet after the final farewell from the great leader, unable or unwilling to carry on as before. Watson is one of the rare exceptions. Under Watson, IBM became the stuff of corporate and stock market legend, continuing to dominate long after Watson's death.

IBM: an example in practice

Thomas Watson created a corporate culture and a corporate brand which lasted. IBM ('Big Blue') became the archetypal modern corporation and its managers the ultimate stereotype – with their regulation sombre suits, white shirts, plain ties, zeal for selling and company song. Their clean-cut, serious professionalism rubbed off on the company's image. IBM was perceived by customers and investors as a sturdy, hardworking company. At an early stage in its development, products, service and employees became intermingled. Dividing lines were blurred so that IBM became an established brand very quickly.

The culture was based on a belief in competing vigorously and providing quality service. Later, competitors complained that IBM's sheer size won it orders. This was only partly true. Its size masked a deeper commitment to managing customer accounts, providing service and building relationships. These elements were established by the demanding perfectionist, Watson.

'He emphasised people and service – obsessively', noted Tom Peters in *Liberation Management*. 'IBM was a service star in an era of malperforming machines.'

IBM's origins lay in the semantically challenged Computing-Tabulating-Recording Company which Watson joined in 1914. Under Watson the company's revenues doubled from $4.2 million to $8.3 million by 1917. Initially making everything from butcher's scales to meat slicers, its activities gradually concentrated on tabulating machines which processed information mechanically on punched cards. Watson boldly renamed the company International Business Machines. This was, at the time, overstating the company's credentials though IBM Japan was established before the Second World War. (The lesson here might be to match your company name to your aspirations rather than your current reality.)

IBM's development was helped by the 1937 Wages-Hours Act which required US companies to record hours worked and wages paid. The existing machines couldn't cope and Watson instigated work on a solution. In 1944 the Mark 1 was launched, followed by the Selective Sequence Electronic Calculator in 1947. By then IBM's revenues were $119 million and it was set to make the great leap forward to become the world's largest computer company.

While Thomas Watson Senior created IBM's culture, his son, Thomas Watson Junior (1914-1994) moved it from being an outstanding performer to world dominance. Watson Jr brought a vision of the future to the company which his father had lacked. Yet, the strength of the original culture remained intact. Indeed, Watson Jr fleshed it out, creating a framework of theories round the intuitive and hard-nosed business acumen of his father.

Typically, Watson Sr made sure his son served a brief apprenticeship, as an IBM salesman, and Watson Jr remained driven by his father's lessons throughout his career. 'The secret I learned early on from my father was to run scared and never think I had made it', he said. And, sure enough, when IBM thought it had made it the ground opened up beneath its previously sure feet.

In his book, *A Business and Its Beliefs* – an extended IBM mission statement – Watson Jr tellingly observes: 'The beliefs that mould great organisations frequently grow out of the character, the experience and the convictions of a single person.' In IBM's case that person was Thomas Watson Senior.

The lessons from IBM are as follows:

- Culture and brand are interlinked: the divide between the two should be transparent. If there is a divide it may undermine the value of the brand. If IBM's service had been poor it would clearly have reflected on the standing of the brand.

- You need to create your own ambitions: at an early stage in the company's development Thomas Watson set out the company's ambitions – putting the word 'International' before the company name was bold and, at the time, rather stretching a point.

- Avoid complacency: the very culture which had made IBM great, based on steadiness, size and reliability, proved its undoing. In the fast moving 1980s, IBM appeared a behemoth, slow moving and out of touch with consumers. Brands do not have a life or a momentum of their own, any momentum they have developed is created by people.

Change and culture

Most of the extensive theorising and practice in the field of achieving change in any organisation pays scant attention to the concerns and fears of the people involved in making it happen. Talk of turbulence and the relentless progress of change through global business is easy. Talk of the effects of upheaval and change on individual managers and employees is less straightforward, fraught as it is with fears and disappointment.

The challenge was described by Niccolò Machiavelli:

'It should be borne in mind that there is nothing more difficult to arrange, more doubtful of success and more dangerous to carry through than initiating changes in a state's constitution. The

innovator makes enemies of all those who prospered under the old order and only lukewarm support is forthcoming from those who would prosper under the new.'

If brands are to be utilised to their full potential this requires changing people's attitudes, beliefs and values. If it is to work, brand management must involve and alter the perceptions and behaviour of people.

The lengthy catalogue of failed change and quality programmes is testament to the general neglect of the people side of such initiatives and, when it is identified, of the failure of organisations to come to terms with it. A survey by KPMG Management Consulting of top executives in 250 UK companies found that only 31 per cent believed their change programmes were 'very effective'.[1] 'Identifying the need for change is relatively straightforward, what really causes problems is making change happen successfully', the KPMG survey reports.

To be effective, change has to carry people along with it. The 'lukewarm support' described by Machiavelli will stop any change programme in its tracks. A programme which looks good in the boardroom can remain a theoretical ideal if people do not commit themselves to the change process.

It is unlikely that successful cultural change can be made in a wholesale way. The past is not easily dismissed, nor should you want to totally dispense with some of the more positive and established ways of thinking and working. Marrying the old and new cultures is a formidable balancing act.

Engineering company Whessoe had, over its 200 years existence, formed a formidable reputation for quality engineering. As its business developed so did the basic premise (its recipe) that the highest possible quality was the core of the business; everything else would then fall into place. Under a new management team the company has, since 1990, begun the process of re-inventing itself and its culture.

It withdrew from its traditional business and moved into instrumentation. It also dispensed with age-old demarcation. Now, shopfloor workers have the same terms and conditions as the rest of the staff – the result has been an end to demarcation disputes. The trouble faced by Whessoe, and many other businesses in traditional industries, is that by recreating itself in a new market it runs the risk of distancing itself from its past achievements and reputation.

Whessoe has managed to combine continuity with radical change. 'One of the dangers ... is that you can lose a lot of the knowledge acquired by the business over many years', says chief executive Chris Fleetwood. The board now includes two directors steeped in experience of the old culture.

> *'Management in industry tends to underestimate what is possible. We tend to look for incremental improvements of five or ten per cent. But in instrumentation it is possible to make those quantum leaps of 200 per cent and that I feel is where our future should be',*

says Fleetwood.[2]

If the real power of brands is to be achieved organisational change is almost always a prerequisite for success. More dauntingly, such transformation is often more easily managed by an outsider or a new chief executive.

KEEPING THE BRAND FRESH

One of the problems often faced by companies is that the initial culture is difficult to sustain. Great ideas hit the market, succeed and then often run out of steam. Keeping fresh is a major challenge – for the organisation, the people and the brand. Often keeping the brand fresh – through new gimmicks, added extras, new campaigns – is the top priority. But it can only be freshened if the organisation is also keeping fresh and on the ball.

SMH, the company marketing the 'Swatch' range of products, has achieved remarkable success by applying creative marketing principles. While other Swiss watchmakers went bust, Swatch learned lessons from other businesses. It made colourful and cheap watches which became fashion accessories. If it had simply tried to copy what others in the same business did it would have probably vanished into the corporate graveyard.

In 1993, around 18 million Swatch watches were produced and the company launches up to 150 designs each year. It has become more than a disposable fashion item, Swatch products have been sold at auctions for £20,000 and there is an international club of collectors with 100,000 members. Swatch continues to do things differently. When it launched its 'Chandelier' model UK sales were restricted to 1,000. The company hired a shop in Covent Garden and sold the 1,000 watches by 4 pm – people travelled from Europe, the US and the Far East for the launch.

> *'As a consequence of Swatch being one of the biggest brands in the world, it tends to be a serious business. That in itself is dangerous because the product is fun. We remind ourselves of that on a daily basis to ensure that the marketing does not lose the spontaneity and flexibility',*

says John Haynes, divisional director of Swatch UK.[3]

The best means of maintaining freshness and originality within a brand or a portfolio of brands is to identify and sustain a set of brand values which are credible and which reflect the culture of the organisation.

At Levi Strauss & Co, ethics and values are not an afterthought; concepts bolted on to the business when economic success is guaranteed. They are at the core of its culture and are perceived to be key drivers of business success. Interestingly, other strong brands such as Marks & Spencer in Britain, Robert Bosch in Germany and Tata Industries in India, have a lengthy tradition of good ethics and values which have shaped and formed their cultures and corporate brands.

> **The best means of maintaining freshness and orginality within a brand or a portfolio of brands is to identify and sustain a set of brand values which are credible and which reflect the culture of the organisation.**

'The importance of such historical commitment cannot be underestimated. A culture of ethics, values and social responsibility is built over time rather than overnight', says former Levi's manager and consultant, David Logan.

> *'Just as the Watsons influenced the culture of IBM so the Haas and Koshland families influenced the ethics and values of Levi Strauss & Co. The company has been a family-owned business for most of its 140-year history and this connection has been critical in shaping its sense of values.'*

As Levi Strauss has expanded it has exported its values alongside. It now draws over 40 per cent of its revenues from its international businesses and sources product from over 50 countries worldwide. Levi's has a worldwide *Code of Ethics* which is based on four key elements:

- A commitment to commercial success in terms broader than merely financial measures.
- A respect for our employees, suppliers, customers, consumers and stockholders.
- A commitment to conduct, which is not only legal but fair and morally correct in a fundamental sense.
- Avoidance of not only real but the appearance of conflict of interest.

Support the brand differently

It makes more sense to support brand leaders with advertising rather than price promotions as their lower price elasticity means the increase in sales from price cutting may not add up to profits.

Most companies aren't able to finance expensive television commercials in the middle of prime time T.V. programmes. Instead, they have limited budgets which they must use to the best effect to support their particular brand. Increasingly, companies are looking for more original means of supporting the brand than conventional advertising:

- Advertising at the bottom of a golf hole: a growing market made attractive to advertisers as it targets middle-aged males. Glenmorangie whisky, Mercedes Benz dealers, Forte Crest hotels and Lloyds Bank are among the companies which have advertised at the bottom of holes on the golfing greens.

- Putting the message on eggs: there is a company called Eggvertising which specialises in advertising on eggs. BT used eggs to promote its daytime rate. It is quirky but when you consider that 98 per cent of households actually buy eggs, not to be dismissed.

- Floor space: supermarkets are notable for their huge expanses of slippery flooring. Now a company called Floor Media is promoting the use of ceramic blocks on supermarket floors featuring and advertising products.

BUILDING FROM CRISES

In 1986 the Rhine was polluted from Schwizerhalle, site of a warehouse owned by Sandoz, Switzerland's second largest chemical company. Soon after the disaster, Marc Moret, Sandoz's chief executive, said that even worse than the material damage 'are the intangible effects which can never be assessed in financial terms – the damage to the Rhine and the deep inroads into the confidence we enjoyed'.

In 1990 Perrier discovered traces of benzene in its bottled water. It had developed a crisis management plan in 1985 which was subsequently put into effect. It quickly regained 86 per cent of its distribution outlets. Even so, Perrier's management maintained for a considerable time that its mineral water did not contain any toxic element in spite of overwhelming evidence to the contrary. The problem was eventually acknowledged – by then the damage had been done.

At some time or another, every manager, every organisation and every brand will encounter a crisis. Some are major world incidents which attract newspaper coverage as surely as magnets attract iron filings. Others are small local difficulties which, if handled badly, accelerate into full-blown disasters.

According to crisis management expert, Lex Van Gunsteren, crises can be divided into two camps: those caused by management which could have been anticipated, and 'unpleasant surprise' crises which are unexpected and totally out of your control. Into the latter category come things like wars, changes in government policies and natural disasters.

Golden rules

In handling any kind of crisis the golden rules are as follows.

Action speaks louder than words

In the age of the soundbite it is tempting to push a spokesman in front of the cameras and have him or her explain the company's deep regret about the unforeseen and completely unexpected crisis. Such platitudes come easily, but they do not solve the problem. It is far better to explain quickly and simply what the company is doing to solve the problem.

In the case of the Pentium flaw, Intel made the mistake of talking rather than acting. Its initial statements played down the flaw. Only later did it act, offering replacements to customers. It would have been much better to offer replacements in the first place while still stressing the relative insignificance of the flaw.

Think long term

It is easy to become bogged down in the minute-to-minute business of solving the crisis. Clearly, this is important. But the organisation needs also to have an eye to the long term. Solving the problem may be highly expensive, but this decision has to be gauged against the long-term business benefits.

Senior managers must take responsibility

The public affairs department must engage operating managers, as well as lawyers, when preparing public statements. Equally, at the earliest possible time, senior managers must take responsibility and be seen to be acting decisively.

After a British Midland plane crashed on the MI the company chairman was at the scene and on television screens as soon as it began to be reported. He was sensitive, honest and decisive. This played a key role in people's perception of the disaster and the company's role.

Communicate internally

Employees have a crucial role to play in bringing the crisis to a speedy practical resolution and in ensuring that it is not repeated. Both these elements can only be achieved through effective, timely and constant communication.

Be proactive

The company has to make the running. If you are continually responding to accusations, however fantastic, it undermines your own position. You can be proactive by communicating regularly and setting the agenda. As the crisis develops, the coverage is as likely to concentrate on your response to the disaster as the actual event.

To be proactive you have to keep up-to-date with how the media is covering the crisis. If it is concentrating on a particular angle, you have to produce a quick and accurate response.

Communication, therefore, must be as honest and open as possible. You should not speculate or become involved in trading allegations and counter allegations. You must consider how others view your action or inactivity. However you act is open to misinterpretation. If you are slow to respond, people may assume you are trying to hide something.

It is better, therefore, to disclose information and the company's position as fully as possible. Silence in any area, or a cagey response mentioning legal restraint is likely to lead to more intense questioning.

Such advice is helpful, but of little value when the required conduct is not in line with the corporate culture, when it does not fit naturally with the prevailing norms and values.

Lex van Gunsteren points out that there are, of course, many examples of the right action being taken. The company which, at great cost, withdrew its oranges from the market when it became clear that a lunatic was injecting them with poison, was rewarded with great customer loyalty once the criminal was caught.

Crises of some sort are inevitable in the life of each and every brand. Most are easily resolved. Others may attract media attention. It is then that the culture of the company and the values of both the organisation and the brand are truly tested.

USING INFORMATION TECHNOLOGY TO BUILD BRANDS

If organisations are to be more effectively geared to managing brands, IT has a vital role to play. While this is easily said, the fact is that, despite massive investments in IT, it is often used for the wrong jobs. Quality programmes, for example, have often exacerbated this situation to the extent that IT becomes marginalised. Instead of being regarded as a core tool by which quality and improved productivity can be achieved, IT has been treated simply as a means of collecting data and ensuring that quality processes are backed by sound statistics.

In the sphere of brands, IT can play a vital role in bridging divides between functions internally and, externally, between companies and retailers.

Part of the problem is that IT is sometimes regarded as a data-gathering device and little else. Unquestionably, IT is the best possible tool for organisations to gather a huge range of data about their brands, customers and overall performance. The crunch comes when data is turned into information – this requires that companies have the systems, processes and people in place to ask the right questions to convert data into information. Data remains data until you ask a question. Information is the answer to the question.

While IT has been used as a means of data-gathering, the emphasis of its practical use has also been on managing the links between different divisions, functions and activities rather than with customers. IT has traditionally looked at what departments do and then provided them with information. It has made an organisation's internal life and systems easier to handle rather than providing improved service to customers.

Often IT is backed by an individual department or function which identifies ways by which IT can make its work more efficient. These do not, however, necessarily apply across the entire organisation. The end result is a number of different systems emerging with little in the way of linkages between them or overall strategy.

'Companies must remain flexible in their IT strategy. Those that declare that open systems are the only way forward may be left in the wake of the Windows rush. Technicians are fond of declaring which is the best operating system but that often has little to do with its success or failure in the market',

says Kevin Grumball, of computer consultants Software Design & Construction. 'It is essential that any IT strategy embraces all the aims of the company rather than taking a parochial view.'[4]

The conventional approach to IT fails to see it in broader strategic terms. IT is regarded as a means of doing existing jobs faster. The obvious corollary of this is that organisations often make the same mistakes at twice the speed.

Companies should be asking themselves:

- How does IT link us to customers?
- How do we measure the productivity gains brought by IT?
- Is IT managed and controlled by a single function?
- Has IT provided us with data or information?

- How has IT helped provide customers with better service?
- How does IT build the brand?

Information Technology enables information to be put simultaneously in the hands of those who need to know, regardless of function or location and enables organisations to break the sequential nature of functional processes for radical improvements in productivity.

> '*In most cases, the greatest practical strategic leverage of IT lies not in some IT-driven company overhaul from top-to-bottom, but in the ability of IT to support the re-design of a company's working practices – that is, its established routines, procedures, techniques and approaches for accomplishing core tasks and activities – as well as its organisational structures*',

say Richard Heygate and Greg Brebach of management consultants McKinsey.[5]

Some examples of IT at work

Clearly, IT should be one of the key tools of any business which genuinely wishes to move closer to its customers, and brands can be seen as a means of becoming closer to customers. Many organisations have already succeeded in using different aspects of IT to provide imaginative solutions and create opportunities and a few examples are discussed below.

Responsiveness

Frank's Nursery and Crafts in Detroit can supply additional stock to its stores when the weekend weather forecast is good. It uses IT to anticipate demand.

US retailer Wal-Mart approached Procter & Gamble, pointing out that it should remind Wal-Mart when to reorder as P&G knows its business and customers better. As a result, P&G manages and finances the Pampers inventory thanks to direct links between Wal-

Mart's checkout system and P&G's ordering system.

Customers of the Dutch PTT can sort out the installation of a new telephone with a single visit to one of the company's offices. This includes a contract, a new number, and the time of connection – now made within two days as opposed to the previous two weeks. By 1995 connections will be made on the spot. Dutch PTT achieved this level of responsiveness by taking the information from its huge mainframe computers and channelling it to individual terminals in sales offices. Instead of switching from one system to another to find all the relevant information, such as on debtors, operators can now locate it easily and quickly.

The IT system used by the Florida-based Home Shopping Network is such that its data is updated every ten seconds. This means that the presenters on television who are selling the products can see how well each is doing. If the charming ceramic rhino is selling badly they can move on to the truly amazing electronic gadget. With this system, HSN can calculate its performance in 'dollars per minute'.

Flexibility

HSN answers customer orders with a recorded voice called 'Tootie'. The computerised system will take people's orders, sort out how they are going to pay and instruct the warehouse to despatch the product to their home address. Not all customers like the idea of speaking to a computer, even one called Tootie. But if the customer does not speak to Tootie within five seconds, her dulcet tones are immediately replaced by a live operator.

Improving performance

The US's Federal National Mortgage Association (Fannie Mae) found that its huge computer system simply could not cope with the growth of its business. In response, it broke down time-consuming departmental divides and installed a network of 2,000 PCs with new easy-to-use software. Costing $10 million, it was a sizeable investment and it paid for itself in less than a year. Though volume doubled between 1991 and 1993, the company took on a mere 100 extra people to cope with the soaring demand. In 1993 Fannie Mae's profits reached $1.87 billion thanks to the company serving a record 3.3 million families through mortgage purchases and security guarantees.

MOVING CLOSER TO CUSTOMERS AND SUPPLIERS

'We know exactly where we want to go, because our customers will show us the way. Our customers know the solutions they need. It's our job to bring them solutions, through the application of technology', says Jerre Stead, chief executive of AT&T Global Information Solutions.[6]

IT bridges gaps between organisations and their customers. DuPont no longer expects invoices from some of its vendors. Instead, it just processes bills electronically. With about 5 per cent of its suppliers the company doesn't even bother with purchase orders. Outside suppliers are linked electronically with DuPont's internal inventory system. When suppliers see DuPont is running short on an item they deliver replacement goods.

> *'Most large organisations are now seeing IT as one of the most important bridges to enhancing customer service. They now rarely see customer service as having separate components, such as marketing, selling, after-sales service and invoicing, each with their own system',*

says Merlin Stone, visiting professor at Kingston University and a partner in Avanti Consultancy Services.[7]

But moving closer to customers and suppliers is not only a key function of IT. It must be a key function of the entire organisation. Understanding customers must be the first step in producing brands they will purchase. Customers can only be understood through close and constant communication and contact.

Customers are demanding more

The interweaving of clients, customers, consumers and other end-users is symptomatic of the growing complexity of relationships between organisations and those who buy and use their products and services. Parallel to this is the increasingly complex nature of customer demand for both consumer and industrial goods. Consider the case of a retail chain which seeks to co-ordinate the activities of promotion, manufacture, warehousing, logistics, procurement, supply and direct product pricing from its suppliers. Functional approaches which serially process the customer through these activities are inappropriate as the nature of the demand is simultaneous.

Quality in respect to customer service is critical to effective business processes. Abrupt changes in the business environment often means that incremental change is insufficient. Quality guru J.M. Juran believes that 80 per cent of problems encountered in organisations can be put down to systems and the remaining 20 per cent to people. Systems, therefore, must be truly customer-oriented, run by people who fully understand the processes they are involved in and who are trained to carry out many different tasks within the process.

Customers are demanding much more. When US aircraft maker Boeing asked its customers what they would like in the new Boeing 777, they requested it should have galleys and toilets which could be relocated anywhere in the cabin within hours. In May 1995 when the first Boeing 777 was produced, the owners were able to rearrange the aircraft within hours, configuring it with one, two or three passenger classes to fit the market at the time.[8]

The development of the 777 is an excellent example of an organisation being forced, through the growing competitiveness of its markets, to make basic changes in its approach. When it began developing the 777, Boeing recognised that it was lagging behind its competitors. McDonnell Douglas and Airbus had a substantial head start. 'We knew how to build aircraft but not how to operate them. We had to learn how to think like an airline', says Boeing's Ron Ostrowski. Boeing radically altered its product design process. Instead of performing design and development tasks sequentially it began running them in parallel. Functions were displaced by design teams which also included customers. Ideas from a British Airways team, for example, helped the Boeing designers install an extra 12 seats making the 777 more attractive to potential customers.[9]

Customers want involvement, choice and the latest technology can give. Therefore, companies have to change their offerings quickly and frequently. Customers demand products which meet their needs, delivery when they want it and easy payment arrangements. This means people who can make operational decisions well down the line, people who do not mindlessly carry out repetitive processes or give standard answers or exhibitions of helplessness when facing customer queries.

The brand does not stop at the factory gate or at the office door, but revolves around continuous relationships and links with stakeholders wherever they are inside or outside the company.

Achieving and monitoring customer satisfaction

Most companies assume that they know what their customers want. Few bother to ask more than the most basic questions about customer satisfaction. If and when they do they are often surprised; customers frequently have a unique and detailed insight into how their supplier works and organises itself. Suppliers, too, are similarly neglected. It is increasingly recognised that organisations are missing a major opportunity; it has been estimated that companies spend around 50 per cent of total production costs on suppliers. The Chartered Institute of Purchasing and Supply estimates that some businesses could be spending up to a third more than necessary on suppliers.

South London plastics company Hunter Plastics found that its customers emphasised service and profits rather than, as Hunter assumed, price and quality. The market research prompted Hunter to develop closer relationships with its customers. Buyers from customers' organisations have subsequently visited the company's factory to discuss issues that concern them and products have been developed to meet their requirements more accurately and consistently. The end result is that Hunter Plastics is now the single source of supply for some customers in particular product ranges.

Partnership sourcing

The entire process of building closer relationships between customers and suppliers has become known as partnership sourcing. Its origins lie in large multinationals buying supplies from smaller companies. Companies like Glaxo, Kodak, IBM, Nissan and British Airways, for example, are all champions of the approach.

Computer company ICL has nearly 200 suppliers signed to its vendor accreditation scheme. The programme arose from analysis which showed that of 6,500 suppliers, ICL did 70 per cent of its business with a mere 200. Suppliers in the accreditation programme have to achieve high quality standards and are subject to performance evaluations by ICL. They are also expected to link up directly with ICL's electronic trading system and, increasingly, to deliver components directly to the production line. ICL's relationships are such that it shares research and development and formulates joint marketing strategies with its leading software supplier.

As in so many instances, Japan is a rich source of best practice. Toyota, for example, manufactures only a third of its needs in-house. It calls on 300 contractors who are at the top level of its tiered supplier structure and who work closely with Toyota. They are also members of its product development teams. The top tier of suppliers then contract out much of the work to smaller suppliers. All the way down the supplier chain, companies are linked by their recognition that working together is a situation which benefits all sides.

A 1993 survey of 280 of the leading European companies by consultants Booz Allen & Hamilton found that 60 per cent of those interviewed insist on a regular presence at their suppliers, compared with 40 per cent five years previously. The consultants anticipate the figure will soon rise to 75 per cent. In addition to this, companies are reducing their supplier base at more than 3 per cent a year, a figure which Booz anticipates will double. BA, for example, had 10,000 significant suppliers in the 1980s – a figure which has now been reduced to 3,500 and is set to fall further. Booz's research suggested that the best performing companies are those moving to 'lifetime' agreements or long-term contracts with suppliers. Interestingly, the best also appear to make the most of fewer resources. In many cases the smaller the purchasing department, the more impressive the performance in terms of material costs, material quality and inventory turnover.[10]

The attractions of partnership sourcing are persuasive:

- Adversarial relationships between buyers and suppliers are replaced by ones of mutual support and benefit.
- Large companies can keep costs down by committing themselves to buying greater amounts from smaller suppliers.
- The customer-supplier relationship can be one of mutual learning with both sides benefiting from an external and new perspective on their business.
- Product development is more likely to match customer needs if the customer's business is more fully understood by the supplier.
- Product development is likely to be faster.

It is also worth noting that partnerships are more likely to prosper between organisations which have shaken off narrow functional approaches. An organisation which finds it difficult to communicate quickly and effectively internally is unlikely to be able to manage a successful relationship with an outside organisation of any sort, especially one that can seem, to the traditionally-minded, intrusive.

'In a partnership it is unlikely that both parties will have equivalent power', says Roger Pudney, of Ashridge Management College, who has carried out extensive research into customer-supplier partnerships across the world.

'But, both parties should be bringing something very distinct to the relationship which the other partner needs. Traditional adversarial type relationships lead companies to exercise their power to gain advantage over their competitors, suppliers and cus-

tomers; in more collaborative relationships this attitude has to be put to one side.'[11]

There are also commercial risks in relation to partnership sourcing. Sharing information, for example, requires high levels of mutual trust. Companies reliant on a single supplier run the risk of their supplier going out of business or attempting to take advantage of the relationship by increasing prices to unacceptable levels.

With rising competitive pressures, it is likely that partnership sourcing will become more widely practised. Organisations which overlook its possibilities are missing an opportunity to share valuable knowledge and experience, and to move closer to both customers and suppliers.

UTILISING DESIGN

'Every company is investing in design to some degree, perhaps unconsciously. Most companies have buildings – shops, factories, workshops, social facilities; communications and information systems – logos, a corporate range of stationery, a corporate brochure, an annual report and accounts, marketing material; perhaps products which they make or buy to sell-on, and product identities or, in the case of some service industries, grander expressions of who they are and what they do',

says Raymond Turner design director of BAA.

The British have a curiously ambivalent attitude to design. Typically, during the eighties, the average manager in charge of overseeing a company's identity lasted approximately nine months. Often, companies continue to regard design as an optional extra, a peripheral activity worth indulging in when things are going well, but generally adding little to commercial success. 'Many British companies still regard design as pretty but dispensable', says Paul Southgate of design consultancy Wickens Tutt Southgate. 'In countries like Italy, however, there is an intuitive understanding of the importance of creativity in business.'

What does design provide?

At a basic level, design provides the means of identification which ensures that the consumer recognises a certain company's products or services anywhere in the world. So IBM or Sony stamped on a product in Tokyo will be as recognisable to a visitor from Helsinki as to one from London.

Design also creates the environment, the setting for the identity. This is a more sophisticated concept and gives designers the opportunity to express the culture and values of the organisation. This creative element has given the world Coke's swirl, Castrol's red, green and white colour palette and BP's solid green and yellow.

> *'Some of the most expensive and comprehensive identity programmes make no visible change to the mark at all. The value of an established, well-recognised mark outweighs even tired-looking original graphics. The Ford logo, for example, is not particularly visually pleasing but it has enormously high recall with consumers',*

says Terry Tyrrell, chairman of Sampson Tyrrell.

> *'It is far easier to bring an old mark up-to-date with incremental change than it is to imbue a new mark with established values. Kodak and Shell have both managed quite major visual change but, because this has been implemented gradually over several years, consumers have been affected only by what they perceive as a sharper, more contemporary overall image.'*

Recognition builds brands and means extra sales. The message is that creativity brings measurable results, Southgate's consultancy gained industry awards for its work in redesigning packaging for the Japanese toy company Tomy. Its new-look products led to a 22 per cent increase in market share, despite increasing the price and cutting advertising spending.

Even with such success stories, in the UK at least, design is still having to fight old battles to prove the case for commercial design excellence.

'The design medium is uniquely powerful. It is a skill, a profession, a discipline which operates across a vast spectrum of media touching every aspect of commercial, social and personal life; from corporate identity to fashion, from theatre design to product packaging',

says Robert Moberly, managing director of design consultancy Lewis Moberly.

'In total order of marketing costs, design is not expensive. It is, in fact, a bargain. The problem is that it tends to be judged not in terms of its effectiveness, but in terms of its cost, and this will continue until designers can persuade clients of its value.'

Future internationalisation

As business becomes increasingly international design businesses are well placed to seize the opportunity. 'It is a relatively young business so people have grown up thinking in pan-European terms', says Paul Southgate. While the advent of the Single European Market opened up areas for many new businesses, design was already thoroughly international.

The global scope of Lewis Moberly's business is typical of the international outlook of the design business. Its track record covers new packaging for a Swedish mineral water; an updated identity for Italian patisserie brand, Le Tre Maria; and work on a range of French yoghurts.

Cultural idiosyncracies provide a rich source of commercial pitfalls. Designers need to know that purple means death in Spain and black is the ultimate premium colour in Italy. Red is masculine in France while in Switzerland yellow is associated with cosmetics – this changes to green in France, Holland and Sweden. In Britain, consumers have been buying mayonnaise in a jar for decades, they are uninterested in how it is made or the recipe. In Italy, mayonnaise had traditionally been homemade and consumers are riddled with guilt as they approach the mayonnaise jars in the supermarket. This is where design steps in. The Italian packaging is radically different, emphasising the ingredients and domestic environment. Guilt is assuaged and a purchase is made.

Managing design

Design requires management. Again companies and brand managers need to be proactive.

> *'The key to harnessing the power of identity is just that – harness it. Left to itself an organisation's identity will certainly develop, but towards visual anarchy rather than clarity. The messages it communicates will gradually become diluted, unclear and even conflicting as individuals – aided and abetted by tools such as desktop publishing – change, adapt or otherwise misuse it at will,'*

says Terry Tyrrell.

> *'Management is crucial. Begin by defining the messages to be communicated through your identity then move heaven and earth to ensure that these are consistently communicated to and by the entire organisation at every point of contact. Make someone at director level responsible for managing it on an ongoing basis. Protect it legally and document its use in such a way as to inspire rather than hobble. Appoint outside help when necessary – and always, always put your head above water at regular intervals to be sure that the identity is still fit for both company and market-place. If you manage all of this you should have developed an identity which can act as a powerful competitive differentiator, a valuable internal motivator and a persuasive corporate ambas-sador.'*

Notes

[1]   KPMG, *Change Management*, KPMG, 1993.
[2]   Levi, J., 'Whessoe's culture change works wonders', Management Today, May 1993.
[3]   Quoted in Wayland, H., 'Marketing time', *Address*, Spring 1994.

[4] *Financial Times*, 14 December 1993.

[5] Heygate, R., & Brebach, G., 'Rethinking the corporation', McKinsey Quarterly, No. 2 1991.

[6] Advertisement in *Financial Times*, 27 January 1994.

[7] Fisher, A., 'Speed is of the essence', *Financial Times*, 3 August 1993.

[8] Peters, T., 'About turn on integration', *Independent on Sunday*, 5 December 1993.

[9] Wheatley, M., *Boeing Boeing*, Business Life, December 1993/January 1994.

[10] Dickson, T., 'A source of best practice', *Financial Times*, 20 August 1993.

[11] Pudney, R., 'The power of partnerships', Directions, September 1993.

BIBLIOGRAPHY

David A. Aaker, *Managing Brand Equity*, The Free Press, New York, 1991.

Sumantra Ghoshal and Christopher Bartlett, *Managing Across Borders*, Hutchinson Books, London, 1989.

Lex Van Gunsteren and Rob Kwick, *Bad Weather Management*, Eburon, Delft, 1991.

David Haigh, *Strategic Control of Marketing Finance*, FT/Pitman, London, 1994.

Paul Hague and Peter Jackson, *The Power of Industrial Brands*, McGraw-Hill, Maidenhead, 1994.

Graham Hankinson and Philippa Cowking, *Branding in Action*, McGraw-Hill, 1993.

Theodore Levitt, *Thinking About Management*, Free Press, New York, 1991.

A.C. Ries and J. Trout, *Positioning: The Battle for Your Mind*, McGraw-Hill, 1981.

Paul Southgate, *Total Branding by Design*, Kogan Page, London, 1994.

INDEX